Word of Faith

Exposing the Critics' Mythology!

Steven Lyn Evans

WESTBOW
PRESS®
A DIVISION OF THOMAS NELSON
& ZONDERVAN

Copyright © 2018 Steven Lyn Evans.

All rights reserved. No part of this book may be used or reproduced by any means, graphic, electronic, or mechanical, including photocopying, recording, taping or by any information storage retrieval system without the written permission of the author except in the case of brief quotations embodied in critical articles and reviews.

This book is a work of non-fiction. Unless otherwise noted, the author and the publisher make no explicit guarantees as to the accuracy of the information contained in this book and in some cases, names of people and places have been altered to protect their privacy.

WestBow Press books may be ordered through booksellers or by contacting:

WestBow Press
A Division of Thomas Nelson & Zondervan
1663 Liberty Drive
Bloomington, IN 47403
www.westbowpress.com
1 (866) 928-1240

Because of the dynamic nature of the Internet, any web addresses or links contained in this book may have changed since publication and may no longer be valid. The views expressed in this work are solely those of the author and do not necessarily reflect the views of the publisher, and the publisher hereby disclaims any responsibility for them.

Any people depicted in stock imagery provided by Getty Images are models, and such images are being used for illustrative purposes only.
Certain stock imagery © Getty Images.

Art Cover Design and interior image credit by Lush Design Studio
www.lushdesignstudio.co.uk
Thanks to Chris Hassler.

The Authorized (King James) Version of the Bible ('the KJV'), the rights in which are vested in the Crown in the United Kingdom, is reproduced here by permission of the Crown's patentee, Cambridge University Press.

Scripture taken from the New King James Version®. Copyright © 1982 by Thomas Nelson. Used by permission. All rights reserved.

ISBN: 978-1-9736-3822-3 (sc)
ISBN: 978-1-9736-3824-7 (hc)
ISBN: 978-1-9736-3823-0 (e)

Library of Congress Control Number: 2018910511

Print information available on the last page.

WestBow Press rev. date: 08/19/2019

Contents

Introduction xiii

Chapter 1: A summary of references and mythology 1
   Introduction 1
   Serious issues for the critics 6
   The Perriman Report 11
   Atonement theology 12
   The mythology in summary 13

Chapter 2: Some of the people involved 15
   Daniel McConnell 15
   Hank Hanegraaff 18
   Justin Peters 21
   Robert Bowman 24
   E. W. Kenyon 25
   Kenneth E. Hagin 26
   Kenneth Copeland 29

Chapter 3: The ministry of Kenneth Copeland 30
   Introduction 30
   Biblical prosperity 31
   Definition of Kenneth Copeland's prosperity doctrine 35
   Foundation principals of Kenneth Copeland's prosperity doctrine. 37
   Influences on Copeland 40
   Copeland's prosperity emphasis 41
   Supernatural prosperity 42
   Purpose of prosperity according to Kenneth Copeland 44

Chapter 4: The 'Word of Faith' movement 46
    What is the 'Word of Faith' movement? 46
    A brief history of the 'Word of Faith' movement 51
    The 'Word of Faith' movement's Pentecostal roots 53
    The 'Word of Faith' movement's supernatural heritage 55
    Kenneth Hagin's influences 61

Chapter 5: McConnell's Mythology 63
    McConnell's mythology of the 'Word of Faith' movement: 63
    McConnell's critique of Kenyan's ministry and influences: 66
    Kenyon is not the Father of the 'Word of Faith' movement 71

Chapter 6: The centrality and commonality of the atonement 74
    Introduction 74
    Issues relating to an assessment of the movement 75
    Why test the atonement doctrine? 76
    Orthodox atonement teaching: A brief survey of doctrines 78
    'Classical' or 'Ransom' theory 78
    'Penal Substitution' or 'Satisfaction' doctrine 80
    'Protestant Orthodoxy' or 'Exchange' doctrine 81

Chapter 7: Kenyon's complex fusion of atonement doctrines 83
    Introduction 83
    Part A: Kenyon's orthodox combination of doctrines 84
    Part B: Jesus Died Spiritually JDS 87

Chapter 8: Redemption Realities 93
    The 'Word of Faith' has a supernatural mission 93
    Supernatural words of faith 95
    Little gods 99
    Personal testimonies 101
    Pastoral emphasis 103
    The love emphasis 105

Chapter 9: Further issues for the critics 107
    Contextualization 107
    Reasons for the 'Word of Faith' movement's missionary success .. 109
    The authenticity of a supernatural emphasis 110
    The critical cessationists 112
    Bowman's classifications 116

Chapter 10: Issues For the 'Word of Faith' movement 118
   Introduction 118
   Balanced prosperity 120
   Healing & troubles 128
   Reasons for troubles in life 130
   Relationships & presumption 131

Conclusion 135
   Breaking through human limitations 135
   It has been shown that: 136
   Further observations from our conclusions 137
   Progressing to prosperity 140
   A global move of God 143
Names and Subject Index 147
Selected Bibliography 157
About the Author 167

Acknowledgments

'But thanks be to God, who gives us the victory through our Lord Jesus Christ' (1 Corinthians 15:57).

For my Mam and Dad, Patricia and Ieuan, thank you for your love and support always in my life. My foundation in God has been helped by your loving examples and my precious family. Thanks to my beautiful darling wife Mikah, whose support and love have been a great ministry to me. Our beloved children Macy and Samual, treasures from above. Martin Newman, whose loving enthusiasm for Jesus, is a testimony that continues to inspire us.

What Christian leaders are saying about this book

Dr. Douglas J. Wingate

Dr. Douglas J. Wingate is President and Founder of the exceptional Life Christian University, based in Florida, USA.

Kenneth Copeland says of Dr. Douglas Wingate & Life Christian University: *"Dr. Wingate, Life Christian University my alma mater, I'm thrilled at the impact you've had on the body of Christ and I am blessed to be a part of it in Jesus' name."*

Joyce Meyer is another worldwide figure of the Christian Church who testifies regarding Dr. Douglas Wingate and Life Christian University: *"I'm honored to be an LCU Graduate, it is an institute of excellence and I'm thrilled to see how God is expanding it so quickly around the world. There is such a need today for intelligent well-informed Christians who not only know what they're talking about but can also relate to people"*

Dr. Douglas J. Wingate writes regarding this book:

I want to highly recommend Dr. Steven Lyn Evans book, "Word of Faith: Exposing the Critics' Mythology!" I have been a Word of Faith teacher and preacher for the past 39 years. I was also mentored by Dr. Kenneth E. Hagin at Rhema Bible Training College and at the daily Healing School services from 1980 to 1982. Even as the President of Life Christian University, I have to admit that I write in common prose to the common reader in order to increase their faith in the Word of God.

What Dr. Evans has produced in his writing is a true apologetic discourse that will even speak to the most critical of academic scholars, while still equipping the sincerely hungry everyday clergyman. Any minister of the gospel must have certainly had altruistic motives of helping others when they answered the call to the ministry. Many ministers also feel extremely deficient when it comes to truly helping those in the midst of the crisis of life. God alone holds all of the answers and solutions to life and its problems, and true and simple faith in His Word brings those solutions into manifestation. I love the words of Dr. T.L. Osborn when he said, "When believed and acted upon, any promise of God is transformed into the power of God. Every Promise of God contains the power of God necessary to produce what it promises, when it is believed and acted upon."

Dr. Evans does an exceptional job of revealing how the lukewarm theology of the critics of Word of Faith, have greatly departed from truly orthodox Christianity and its fundamental tenants of faith. He elaborates on the myths embraced by each of the critics, exposes them and brings us to the conclusion that the Word of Faith movement was, and is still a revival and return to true orthodoxy. I am speaking of 1st Century, Apostolic experience in ones faith in Christ and all of His promises, to those who believe in the power of His Name.

The critics seem to always be non-Pentecostal, non-charismatics who have missed out on the demonstrations of God's power in this generation. My suggestion to every reader is to start there, be baptized in the Holy Spirit, with the evidence of praying in other tongues, the supernatural ability to pray the perfect prayer in every instance. It is then that you will gain the ability to rightly divide the Word of Truth. After this experience, you are going to really enjoy the illumination that comes as you read this exceptional book.

Dr. Douglas J. Wingate,
President and Founder of Life Christian University, Florida, USA

Bishop Tom Brown

Bishop Tom Brown is often known for his deliverance ministry as seen on ABC's 20/20, as well as on MSNBC and the History Channel. He is a noted conference speaker, prolific best-selling author and an international Bishop.

Bishop Brown writes regarding this book:

Bishop Steven Evans is clearly the person to write this defense of the Word of Faith. He embraced it through a thorough study of the movement.

He is a recognized Bishop who holds to orthodox teaching. He clearly lays out in a methodological way the true beliefs and true history of the Word of Faith movement. I wholeheartedly endorse this book.

Bishop Tom Brown
Word of Life Cathedral, Texas, USA

Revd. Melvin Banks

Revd. Melvin Banks the famous English Evangelist has been evangelizing with miracles following in 60 nations of the world for 65 years. He has often been called 'The second Smith Wigglesworth.'

Dr David Yongi Cho, Seoul, Korea says: *"In every generation God has Prepared men of great faith to step into the scene at his appointed time, to call sinners to repentance, and then build his church ... with faith and deliverance. We commend Melvin Banks for years of outstanding ministry throughout the UK and as God's chosen vessel for your land, for this important day and time."*

Revd. Banks writes regarding this book:

"Wells have run dry" in the Western World's Christianity, the amazing, God blessed (so called) Faith Movement, has become a gleaming, shining ray of light to untold millions.

Bishop Steven Evans' inspiring, concise, brilliant and factual defense of this mighty awakening world-wide, is both on-the-dot, timely, absorbing and excellent. A "Must-Have" for every Christian believer and minister. You will not be the same again! A masterpiece! Next to the Holy Bible, don't read any other book this year!

Revd. Melvin Banks
International Evangelist

Introduction

'The further a society drifts from the truth, the more it will hate those that speak it' [Orwell, 2018]. It does seem that at times, the same phrase could be applied to the church. The further the church drifts from the truth, the more it will hate those that speak it.

During my training for ministry at St. Michael's Anglican College in Llandaff, South Wales, I was placed in the community of Bridgend South Wales. It was an interesting time for me personally, but it was a very sad time for that community. The Welsh Assembly recognized 23 suicides between 2007-2008 in that area of Bridgend, these were mostly young men. Personally, I knew of many other young men who had committed suicide from my home region of South Wales. Young men who I had been in school with, some were friends, people with whom I had happy childhood memories.

What had happened to the land of revivals? The Welsh revival of 1904 and the fires of those days were testified to by the array of chapels and churches throughout the nation. What were once happy and overflowing places of worship though, are now often empty, or relegated to providing housing, shops, and restaurants. What a tragedy. Deep inside, I wanted to find answers for the people, to reach them with the Gospel, I wanted to give people hope.

I continued my research into the 'Word of Faith' movement whilst doing post-graduate studies in theology. For me, it was clear, the 'Word of Faith' movement wasn't a mere theological positioning, it was something real that was formulated out of a practical need in people. The 'Word of Faith' movement's leadership, is made up of people who were often once impoverished but they had decided to believe God, and subsequently they had received (Matthew 21:22). It was refreshing to read people who were prepared to believe that the Bible was inspired, that it was and is, the

'Word of God.' This was a long way from the distant approach of most of my college Professors. It encouraged me to believe God again, just as I did when I first came to faith. In the academic world, most of the time, if you believe in the Bible as the 'Word of God,' you're an oddity, you're regarded as somewhat naive. Within Enlightenment based formal theology the Bible is to be critiqued, picked apart, treated with the objective skepticism of Critical Theory. However, within this work it will be shown that this view is often itself impoverished; it leads to people to follow a western based framework of thinking, rather than the Bible. It denies all absolutes apart from its own. It results in people who don't believe in Heaven or Hell, evangelism, miracles, or the joy of salvation through Jesus Christ alone.

I can remember as a boy growing up in South Wales, I was aware of the miraculous legends of the patron Saint David (c.500 – c.589), the Welsh Celtic Bishop. The miraculous life that he lived spoke to me deep inside about the potential of God to manifest through a man. Could it possibly happen, would God do that? I wanted that kind of life, and in the 'Word of Faith' movement, I had found a group of people who were similarly open to the supernatural and miraculous. People of faith, believers in a long historical succession of the faithful, who revered and followed the Holy Bible. People who were genuinely changing the world through the Gospel of Jesus Christ. This gave me an expectancy and hope. I found that ministers such as: Kenneth Hagin (1917-2003), Charles Capps (1934-2014), Kenneth Copeland, Creflo Dollar, Jesse Duplantis, Norvel Hayes, Marilyn Hickey, Joyce Meyer, Keith Moore, T. L. Osborn (1923-2013), David Oyedepo, Fred Price, Bishop Michael Reid, Rick Renner, Jerry Saville, Leroy Thompson, Robert Tilton, Bill Winston and many others, were writing from real life experience, not dry theory. Their books were packed with personal illustrations, they were real, the faith they spoke about was life transforming and world impacting! It was a great inspiration to me in that otherwise mostly dry, theological environment.

I entered my first theological College in London because I was enthusiastic about the Gospel of Jesus Christ and I wanted to learn about how to reach people and help them. I thought that I would be searching the scriptures to find the truth and then my faith would grow. What I experienced in the college, however, was a lot of cynicism, the Bible was continuously questioned, faith in it as authoritative was undermined. It was all too clinical, calculating and distant, rather than devotional. I could see that it was leading many people towards a detachment from their personal devotion to God. An authentic belief was being lost in the cold, calculating, of Critical Theory. My simple desire to learn how to share the Gospel was being lost. After graduating from the College, the sad truth was that I was depressed, I had lost my enthusiasm, I had lost my intrinsic belief system. Why evangelize for example, if you've been indoctrinated into believing that Hell doesn't really exist? What was it all about? After College, there was a growing meaningless to my life.

The change started one day as I lay aching in bed with the flu. The cloud of depression had contributed towards an array of various aches and pains and during this period, a severe bout of influenza. My life was a mess, and despite my head knowledge, I was living in defeat.

There was a knock on the door this one day, and I struggled out of my sickbed to peep through the frosted glass and see who it was. "Oh! No!" I thought, because at the door was Martin Newman, my evangelist friend. He seemed to be always enthusiastic for God and frankly, I thought he was too much for me to cope with in the state I was in. I remember thinking, I hope he hasn't seen me. I turned around crouched down and started walking back to bed. Then I heard him call saying "I can see you, Stevie, let me in!"

I sheepishly turned around and said "No Martin! I'm too ill!"

But he insisted, and so I said, "Just for 5 minutes."

I crept back to bed, and he followed me into the room, he sat at the end of my bed saying,

"I'm going to fill the atmosphere with praise."

I said, "No you're not!"

He said, "I'll just sing very softly."

I said, "I've got an earache.

At that point, if I had enough energy, I might have attempted to throw him out, but he started to sing, and it was softly, so I just laid back and rested, thinking he would soon be finished and leave me in peace. He was singing a chorus with the words: *"Shout to the Lord, shout to the Lord, shout to the Lord of hosts, It breaks the heavy yoke, it breaks the heavy yoke, when we shout, we shout to the Lord."* He just kept repeating these words, again and again, and after about 10 minutes, I started to enjoy the melody, and the words, they were ministering to me. After about 20 minutes, I was beginning to feel a little better, and so much so, that I started to sing along with him gently, the words were having an effect on me. For the first time in a long time, I wasn't focusing on my troubles, sicknesses, and problems, I was just worshipping the Lord.

After about half an hour, I had got out of the sick bed and was standing with my arms raised, praising God. It was a complete transformation, my faith had responded, and received. The result of the words of faith that were being sung, was that the yoke had been destroyed, and I was healed! Just as Jesus had promised: *'hitherto have ye asked nothing in my name: ask, and ye shall receive, that your joy may be full'* (John 16:24). The words we were singing came true, the *'Heavy yoke was broken.'* There was power in these words, this wasn't just a nice tune this was life changing truth. There is an important principle for life here: What you focus on, you'll get direction from.

Now this experience went against a lot of my theological rationale, I wondered what my academic friends would think, they would critique my experience no doubt, but I, like the blind man with Jesus in John 9:25, could now say, that I'd experienced a real physical healing, I'd been healed! Undoubtedly, this was a far better theological rationale, a theology that actually works! This was a practical theology for real life. Not a dry theory, this was living faith! I remember it was like I had become born again, again! However, this time I had an understanding that 'God's Word,' really works, it is true! It's not something dead, to be cut apart, dissected endlessly, and critiqued. Rather, it's living, to be listened too, understood, applied, and held in the highest esteem. It is God's handbook for life: *'For the Word of God is quick (living), and powerful (active), and sharper than any two-edged sword, piercing even to the dividing asunder of soul and spirit, and of the joints and marrow, and is a discerner of the thoughts and intents of the heart'* (Hebrews 4:12).

I was feeling so good after an hour or so, no headaches, earache, pain, or influenza, that I accompanied Martin that night and preached the Gospel on the streets of London! Several people came to know Jesus as Savior that evening, as I gave testimony to the saving, and the healing power of Jesus.

I reflected on that evening the next day, and I realized that I had a decision to make. I could stick to my theological theories and carry on in defeat, or I could continue adopting the perspective of Martin and experience a life of victory. I had an array of questions for Martin, I was skeptical of the 'Word of Faith' movement, all the people I knew were skeptical. However, the professors at the college weren't as happy as Martin, they weren't as enthusiastic about Jesus, they didn't hand out tracts and behave as if the Gospel was the most important thing in life. They didn't ever seem to expect miracles from God, that would be scoffed at. When I looked at Jesus' life and the life of the Apostle Paul, Martin was far closer to that kind of life than the theological lecturers whom I knew. The decision was easy, it was a hinge moment in my life, I asked Martin to show me the books he read and studied because I needed to read and study them also. The Bible was obviously the first book, it was to be read as a manual for life, it contains all the answers to life's questions. Next to the Bible, I can remember being in Hyde Park in central London, when Martin introduced me to Charles Capps' book, 'The Tongue: A Creative Force.' That's where my transformation through the 'Word of Faith' movement really started.

As I continued to read and listen to Hagin, Copeland, Dollar and many others, they were so inspiring, so life-giving, so Bible-believing. For them, the Bible was a book of counsel, a higher authority, not something to be cynically scrutinized but something to direct us and learn from, to be taken very seriously. I remember thinking, at last, people with enough commitment and gumption to say they believe the Bible and they also desire to live by it. It was also inspiring to witness the wealth and success that these ministries enjoyed, it spoke to me of the abundance of God, of His provision for life. Rather than a poverty mindset, these people were living like champions, living victorious, they were living the God-life. They inspired me to believe that God could provide, as soon as I believed that, I started to receive. Just a simple change of mindset did it and that adjustment changed my life. I found out that having friends who don't believe and are cynical, can be very costly.

I was innately suspicious of the pretense of indifference towards prosperity, that often existed in the church. It just didn't ring true, on the most basic human level we want the best for others, we want people to do well and succeed. I would recall for example, my grandfather writing his Christmas cards to people ending with the salutation, 'A very prosperous New Year.' It was so obviously right to desire to prosper, you needed a good dose of error not to see it.

As I was considering this work, I reflected on one of the significant issues that I faced as a theological graduate when I first reviewed the 'Word of Faith' movement. It seemed to have a different approach to the Bible to what I had known. It was bold enough to offer definite answers, it wasn't always trying to show objectivity by perpetually questioning itself. It had no need for egalitarian idealism. In an age where absolutes have become unfashionable, it was offering continuous absolutes through the 'Word of God.' Just imagine, I was a theological College graduate and was surprised to find that people still believed and trusted in the Bible. This was a great blessing and even a revelation to me. The Enlightenment based theology of Critical Theory has been misused so much, that it ultimately undermined the believer from having a devotional adherence too, and belief in, the 'Word of God.' Western theology has become so insular that wider global theological positions which embrace supernatural Biblical experiences, are usually beyond reach.

As I moved into my first Pastoral position, the 'Word of Faith' influence on my thinking caused me to accept Biblical promises regarding healing and miracles. It wasn't long before the church that I Pastored was featured on front page secular newspaper headlines across Britain. There were many testimonies from people of tremendous miracles taking place. These miracles happen as a result of yielding to believe the Bible as authoritative, rather than trusting in your own thinking and past experiences. Apparently, the last time this type of attention was given on front page headlines was through the ministry of Smith Wigglesworth. I was pleased that the remarkable healing evangelist Revd. Melvin Banks, sometimes known as 'The second Smith Wigglesworth,' kindly contributed a recommendation for this work. Revd. Banks' ministry has extensively been featured in the secular press over several decades. Thousands of people have testified to receiving great miracles and healing from God through his ministry.

The 'Word of Faith' movement has brought a significant blessing to the worldwide church, it is turning people all over the world, towards a living faith life. The real impetus behind this work are the thousands of lives that have been changed through the impact of the 'Word of Faith' movement. I've witnessed and had the privilege of being involved in some of these transforming events. I want many others to experience the same blessings that I have, I don't want them to be robbed by the cynics, the mythology pushers, the cessationists. My enthusiasm isn't so much focused on dramatic miracles, although these have been plentiful and are always celebrated, but rather on the deep faith that results in a disciplined day-to-day Christian life.

The 'Word of Faith' movement's name is taken from the Biblical passage of Romans chapter 10 verse 8 which reads, *'...the word of faith that we preach.'* Within the movement, words and faith are both vital in being a new creation in Christ. The New Testament provides many essential Biblical teachings on these key areas, such as: *'Faith comes by hearing and hearing by the word of God'* (Romans 10:17). In addition, human faith is released by the words that we speak, for example: *'...Whosoever shall say unto this mountain, Be thou removed, and be thou cast into the sea; and shall not doubt in his heart, but shall believe that those things which he saith shall come to pass; he shall have whatsoever he saith'* (Mark 11:23). Jesus Christ teaches in this verse, that the words that we speak, when spoken in faith, carry great and transforming power. In accepting Jesus Christ's words as pertaining to a supernatural life today, the 'Word of Faith' movement has broken with religious traditions. We will look at this further within chapter 1, suffice to say that these traditions have either gone against, or been ignorant towards, Biblical truth.

Ultimately, this work is not about theological theory but the Gospel truth and its substantial impact on the everyday life of people. I commit this work to you, therefore, in the hope that we might *'.... Be like-minded, having the same love, being of one accord, of one mind'* (Philippians 2:2).

Chapter 1

A summary of references and mythology

Introduction

The critics' mythology holds to an audacious methodology. They are often both historically and theologically wrong. They have peddled a myth and divided the church. It's time for truth!

The impetus behind this work came from a basic desire to present people with the truth regarding the 'Word of Faith' movement. Millions of people around the world have been positively impacted by the movement. Nevertheless, the critics have not only sowed dissension, they have systematically created a mythology. The Bible clearly warns of such, *'And they shall turn away their ears from the truth, and shall be turned unto fables'* (2 Timothy 4:4). In this case, the fables are found within the critics' mythology, which is often but not always, born out of the heresy of cessationism.

Cessationism denies the Baptism of the Holy Spirit, tongues, miracles, healings, and many other Biblical charismatic practices. Cessationists have adopted a pretense of Biblical adherence, while denying huge portions of the New Testament. As the Perriman Report, commissioned by the British Evangelical Alliance has observed, 'Many evangelicals, while committed to the intellectual truth of the gospel, would prefer to live out their faith within the normal parameters of everyday life' (2003, p.218). In other words, they have no interest in the supernatural reality of a New Testament life. Consequently, from this position they have little ability to understand the 'Word of Faith' movement with its supernatural and Biblical emphasis.

Critics who are not necessarily cessationists, are nevertheless also often from western Enlightenment based schools of theology. As we will see, these are less supernaturalistic in their views. They find it difficult to embrace the supernatural emphasis within the 'Word of Faith' movement. According to Christian anthropologist Charles Kraft, systems of western theological analysis are bound to exclusively Western methodologies and are entirely different to the methods employed by the majority of the rest of the world (1996:88). These methodologies can be traced back to the Enlightenment, and Kraft makes the thought-provoking observation that western theology is 'largely captive to western cultural ways of thinking' (1996:88). This helps to explain why the 'Word of Faith' movement has been attacked so vigorously, the theological paradigms used to assess the movement, have been limited by the prevailing anti-supernatural western theological emphasis.

Authenticity increasingly demands, within a global church, that theology should return towards its original roots and be relevant both towards, and from, ordinary life. In modern history, increasingly, much of theological study has been confined to the theoretical opinions of theologians and significantly divorced from everyday believers' lives. This has contributed towards a lack of supernatural emphasis because it is in the needs of everyday life, that the supernatural finds its essential expression. Jesus' miracles for example, met the supernatural needs of people and He has commissioned believers to do the same (Mark16:15-20). Therefore, this book deliberately includes supernatural examples and real-life testimonies.

This holistic approach is more Eastern and Biblical, it should be differentiated from the linear Platonistic approach, of much within modern western theology. Further, some of the examples and testimonies included within this work, will prove difficult to embrace for those within a modern western mindset. We will show that anthropologists and missiologists have, along with some theologians, recognized significant deficiencies and limitations within western Enlightenment based theology. Nussbaum for example, quotes the noted missiologist Bosch, whose central thesis understood 'that the Enlightenment worldview is a seriously inadequate view of reality.' (2005, p.151). For those within this framework, Nussbaum makes vitally important observations that, 'It is hard to find a German New Testament scholar or theologian who has witnessed a convincing physical healing.' He goes on to point out that it is equally as hard, 'to find a member of a Chinese house church or an African indigenous church,' who has not witnessed a convincing physical healing. In conclusion, he points out that,

'Miraculous physical healing does exactly what the Enlightenment says cannot be done' (2005, p.151).

This reveals the root of the problem for the critics. They are viewing the 'Word of Faith' movement from one side only, it's a limited view but they are convinced they are right. Picture for example, two people sitting on a sofa, with a framed painting in-between them. One person would be correct in describing the object they see as a dull, old, stained wooden board with string dangling in the middle. Their view of the picture is from the back only, from the other side, there is a beautiful array of colors and a scene so wonderful that the persons emotions are deeply stirred. Often the 'Word of Faith' movement's critics, are sincere in describing what they see but their view is limited, they have not seen the full picture. From an Enlightenment based skeptical theology, they never will. To understand the other side, it must be experienced and for that to happen, the confines of limited western theology must be left behind.

This understanding forms part of the foundation of this work, Christianity is supernatural and consequently it must incorporate the supernatural into its theology and worldview. The lack of current supernatural emphasis within western Christianity, demonstrates a lack of Biblical reality and goes a long way towards explaining why so many Enlightenment shaped western denominations, are in serious decline today. This impoverished theological emphasis, denies the legitimate needs of people to engage in supernatural Biblical truth as an expression of their faith. This theological error has created a vacuum, which is often being replaced by other faiths and practices. These willingly embrace and teach their own emphasis of the supernatural, for example, the New Age movement, Witchcraft and Wicca. The Pew Research Center for example, found in 2014 that 0.4% or up to 1.5 million Americans are actively involved in Wicca. That number shows a 400% growth in just 6 years but the same research center at Trinity College in Connecticut, showed that in 1990 the number of Wiccans was only 8,000 (Singh-Kurtz and Kopf, 2019). This rapid growth has taken place during the same timeframe that the 'Word of Faith' critics have gained popularity by often attacking and denying the supernatural. Wiccans recognize the supernatural exists, but the cessationists deny it. The cessationist bias of the 'Word of Faith' critics such as McConnell, MacArthur, Hunt and Peters, has flourished throughout many churches. There is no way to measure the significant extent, of the harm caused by this heresy.

The 'Word of Faith' movement's critics are almost entirely positioned from within an Enlightenment based theological paradigm. For this reason, many will scoff at the 'Word of Faith' movement's position on healing and prosperity. They are often so indoctrinated by their narrow Enlightenment based anti-supernatural worldview, that they cannot even begin to conceive the possibility of 'Word of Faith' Biblically based concepts.

As far as I'm aware, this work is the first to classify the critics of the 'Word of Faith' movement, as having established mythology. I believe this is useful, as it truly summarizes the general compilation of the critics' positions. They have collated a series of myths to compile a systematic mythology. The mythology is therefore exposed by the following facts:

1) A lack of theological support for the critics' claims.
2) The lack of historical accuracy within the critics' claims.
3) The extreme and divisive nature of the critics.
4) The demonstrable erroneous conclusions of the critics.

In proof of the points above, the critics' positions, as we will see within this work, have been undermined by some of the most authoritative historical and theological voices available. There are many specific supportive facts for the 'Word of Faith' movement that could be of important use to a wider audience moving forwards. In addition, a picture will evolve of the movement and its Biblical emphasis.

As we will see, it has been observed that the critics of the 'Word of Faith' movement, have often used the extremes of the movement to define and characterize it. It is beyond the scope of this work to deal with all of these, but we will expose some of the most influential popular criticisms. It is worth noting also that all movements have a propensity to gain people with somewhat polarized expressions. In other words, we could probably conclude that no group of Christians in church history have been devoid of those with a tendency to push towards extremes. The key is not to define movements by those people or their positions but by the truth of the movements more central emphasis. The reality of a movements central thrust.

The often-spurious position of some of the critics is also highlighted by their dominant focus and fixation on the 'Word of Faith' movement itself. Given that in recent church history radical liberal trends have swept into the Christian church, any fair examination of the critics would wonder why, if they are so concerned with error, are they so silent on so many radical, liberal theological trends. These trends have infiltrated the church via the influence of people such as Søren Kierkegaard, Paul Tillich and Rudolf Bultmann. Bultmann for example, argued for an existentialist interpretation of the New Testament in which historical analysis is both futile and unnecessary (Broadhead pp. 1169–1182: 2011). Despite this radical theory, remarkably because Bultmann demonstrates Enlightenment based research criteria, he is taken seriously by western theological theologians. Hagin or Copeland on the other hand, who advocate for Biblical principles would be significantly marginalized. The hypocrisy of this situation ought to be very obvious, but western theology is often blinded in the shadow of the Enlightenment.

Therefore, the 'Heresy hunters' as they have been often known, seem to have avoided the biggest and most wide ranging of heresies that have attacked the Christian church. The radical liberals have eaten away at the core foundations of the faith without any disturbance from so called 'Heresy hunters.' This observation ought to cause serious questions to be asked of the critics and the sincerity of their claims to be the agents of God, defending the church from heresy. In truth, they are more closely aligned with the liberals, in opposing those who claim the Bible as inerrant and a foundation for Christian life today. Further, in a remarkably great irony, they themselves are often filled with those who adhere to the heresy of cessationism.

The main reasons for this book were that there were seriously negative and damaging problems created by the critics that hadn't been addressed. The 'Word of Faith' movement has been mainly silent in the face of the critics. Whilst this approach is admirable to some degree, it is also useful at times to *'reprove, rebuke, exhort with all longsuffering and doctrine'* (2 Timothy 4:2). Part of the aim of this work is to do that, in the hope that some will be saved from the divisive trap of the mythology. For many people the negative critical mythology resulted in the following:

- People believed the mythology of the critics.
- Historical inaccuracies have been accepted as truth.
- Ingrained suspicion of the 'Word of Faith' movement.
- Many Christian groups have become prejudiced against the movement.
- People are less open to God.
- People reject truth and Biblical reality to follow cessationist mythology.
- Churches have been split due to the mythology.
- Peoples spiritual gifts have been suppressed.
- A great and worldwide move of God has been illegitimately undermined.

Rather than allowing the above to continue without challenge, this book seeks to address the mythology, in the hope that people will renew, or find fresh encouragement from the 'Word of Faith' movement and its global network of ministries.

Serious issues for the critics

D. R. McConnell mixed an unhealthy combination of limited history, biased theology, and unconscionable criticisms, to create a mythology aimed at attacking the 'Word of Faith' movement. He attempted to link Revd. E. W. Kenyon to the metaphysical cults and then linked Revd. Kenneth Hagin to Kenyon and the mythology was born.

The mythology claimed that the 'Word of Faith' movement was cultic. Many other critics jumped onto the mythological bandwagon. The most vocal was probably Hank Hanegraaff who took the title of 'The Bible Answer Man.' However, often his efforts have been exposed as being less than his title might suggest. He will be shown to be repeatedly both theologically and historically deficient. DeArteaga for example, has observed that Hanegraaff's arguments lack 'a broad Christian historical perspective' (2001, p.268). He goes on to say that Hanegraaff's views on aspects of the atonement are 'a serious injustice to many Orthodox believers' (2001, p.271). The irony here is utterly remarkable because many years later in 2017, Hanegraaff was to join the Eastern Orthodox Church! This change of emphasis by Hanegraaff is so dramatic, that one might wonder if, perhaps, more irony is still to come and maybe his next work might be a defense of the 'Word of Faith' movement?

One of the most serious issues regarding many of the critics of the 'Word of Faith' movement is that they are cessationists. We will show for example, 'Word of Faith' critics such as McConnell, John MacArthur, Justin Peters and Dave Hunt hold to that belief. Hunt's influential 1985 book 'The seduction of Christianity' is regarded by the Perriman Report as strongly cessationist in its views (2003, p.13). Hunt's position goes against so much within established church history and the Bible. In chapter 4 of this work for example, we cite ministers who prove the supernatural gifts are in operation post-Biblical times: Justin Martyr, Irenaeus the Greek bishop noted for his role in combatting heresy, Justin to Trypho, Tertullian who looked on exorcism as a proof that 'Christ is victorious over the Roman gods,' Origen, Gregory the 'Wonder Worker,' Augustine, Spurgeon, Wesley, Luther and many other modern ministers.

The cessationist position is strongly at variance with the church's established position regarding supernatural manifestations. Also, the Bible is explicit in its expectation of miraculous ministries. Therefore, the cessationists position should be regarded as clear heresy. In effect, these critics attempt to discredit Jesus' words, much within the New Testament and church history itself. McConnell, MacArthur, Peters, Hunt and many of the other critics, are joined in their cessationism by groups such as the Jehovah's Witnesses and Mormonism both of which are strongly opposed to the Biblical teaching on gifts.

Anyone who is seriously interested in the truth regarding the 'Word of Faith' movement will need to engage with the available objective academic appraisals. The British Evangelical Alliance, for example, commissioned 'Faith, Health and Prosperity: A Report on 'Word of Faith and 'Positive Confession' Theologies by ACUTE (the Evangelical Alliance Commission on Unity and Truth among Evangelicals).' In short, the Report is referred to within this work as the Perriman Report, named after its editor Andrew Perriman. The Perriman Report offers perhaps, the most serious scholastic work on the 'Word of Faith' movement to date. Its conclusions, whilst not entirely favorable to the 'Word of Faith' movement, expose critics of the 'Word of Faith' movement in the most serious manner. The report was written from an evangelical perspective rather than 'Word of Faith' and so its conclusions against the critics, are all the more impacting. It contributes significant proof toward the critics having established mythology. Let's take a glimpse at some of those conclusions and some of the main contributing voices:

Firstly, the Perriman Report observed that the critics of the 'Word of Faith' movement have, 'ingrained and largely unexamined moral revulsion' against the movement (2003, p.231). This observation is accurate, and the critics of the 'Word of Faith' movement have what seems to be a pathological animosity against the movement. This is to the degree that often the critics are striking in their theological and historical compromises. In using the word 'unexamined,' the Perriman Report is highlighting the historical tendency that exists with the critics, against the movement. The critics have shown prejudice and what the Perriman Report calls 'spiritual snobbery' (2003, p.231). This has had a significant impact so that even neutral people will often find it more acceptable to criticize the movement than to go against the liberal flow and defend it. This 'spiritual snobbery' is also connected to the formal academic background of many of the critics. Adherents of the 'Word of Faith' movement on the other hand, are not usually from a formal academic background.

Perhaps it is not surprising given the spread of the mythology, that the Perriman Report highlighted significant problems in establishing accurate and balanced appraisals about the movement (Perriman 2003, p.1). The Perriman Report chastises the critics of the 'Word of Faith' movement and suggests that the debate regarding the orthodoxy and roots of the movement 'has been marred by misrepresentation, polarization, and invective' (2003, p.15). It goes on to make the very important observation that critics of the 'Word of Faith' movement, tend to be biased in their use of limited historical and biographical material. This material has, 'frequently been assembled for the purpose of discrediting the movement' (2003, p.1). Further, it recognizes that the critics have created 'caricatures' which it concludes are 'an indiscriminate instrument of polemic' (2003, p.231-4). The creation of 'caricatures' is often done, when one group feels empowered enough to be utterly dismissive of another. The roots of bullying are at times, found in this type of charged environment. In other words, the danger of creating caricatures is that it causes a generalization to take place. This leads to marginalization and a subsequently unfair prejudice grows. This is precisely what the critics were attempting to do in establishing their mythology of Kenyon and the 'Word of Faith' movement. Their generalizations repeatedly fail to engage in the complexity of the fusion of doctrines that exist.

The Perriman Report insightfully observes '...that there is more to the teaching of Hagin and Copeland than is found in the one-sided analysis of their opponents' (2003, p.232). DeArteaga points out that 'the key is recognizing the difference between 'collections' and history; between assembling a scrapbook of errors and writing a fair description of another's theology' (1996, p.269). The Perriman Report has been very clear to point out that some of the critics of the 'Word of Faith' movement have adopted 'polarized positions.' In turn, these have led to unbalanced and extreme classifications of the movement as being 'cultic' (2003, p.15). This is a vitally important point by the most authoritative report ever commissioned.

Bowman, who according to the Perriman Report offers the most academic appraisal, has concluded correctly alongside the Perriman Report, that Hagin is the Father of the movement (2001, p.36). This is a very significant conclusion as it exposes the critics' foundational mythology. This is because, if Hagin is the movements Father, then the invented link connecting Kenyon as the movements Father, is broken. Therefore, the invented connection to the metaphysical cults is exposed. Nevertheless, it will be shown that the claimed connection to the metaphysical cults is entirely spurious on several levels. Similarly, to the Perriman Report,

Bowman also dates the movement's origins to after the Second World War and shows that the movement's roots are to be found, not in the metaphysical cults, but in Pentecostalism (2001, p.7,11,12; 2003, p.77). DeArteaga's critique to Hanegraaff's polarized book, 'Christianity in Crisis' is worth noting; he suggests that: 'Behind its numerous citations and quotations lays a profound methodological error – the assumption that listing the worst errors of a movement is a truthful representation of that movement' (1992, p.269). In one typical example of Hanegraaff's biased mythology, he suggests that the 'Word of Faith' movement sees demons behind 'every bush' and also 'they are behind every disease' (1993, p. 257). This exaggeration is typical of what Hanegraaff offers his readers, he simply adds his own 'colorful and imaginative additions' (Bowman 2001, p.30). The Perriman Report in comparison, has taken care to recognize the truth that the 'Word of Faith' movement has viewed, 'In many cases the persistence of illness is attributed to the activity of demons' (2003, p.47). This more balanced appraisal provides the discerning reader with an entirely different understanding of the movement on this crucial doctrine. Demonic activity does exist, but it is not always claimed by the 'Word of Faith' movement as the reason for all disease. Ultimately, the denouncing of the mythology by the most authoritative voices is unequivocal, the evidence is substantial and ought to be taken very seriously, the implications are important and far reaching into the body of believers worldwide.

DeArteaga accuses McConnell's perspective of coming from a cessationist, anti-charismatic bias. Here we are perhaps striking at the very heart of the mythology, a western theological anti-supernatural bias. He also points out in his response to McConnell, that Kenyon's arguments were used to strengthen the orthodox faith against what he regards as the corrosive effect of higher criticism (Perriman 2003, p.74). Therefore, rather than interpreting Kenyon's doctrines as a watered-down syncretistic gospel suggested by McConnell, DeArteaga has offered a diametrically opposite opinion, showing Kenyon as a clear advocate for recognizable Christian theology.

In responding to the 'Word of Faith' movement's repeated and clear differentiation to the cults, McConnell contests that many within the faith movement issue disclaimers when their doctrines are similar to cults (1988, p.43). In saying this, McConnell is refusing to accept the objective evidence, even when it is historically or theologically factual. If the objective evidence refutes his position, it seems that he is prepared to dismiss it. The Perriman Report offers another insightful and key observation on this issue: 'Similarities do not necessarily indicate dependence, and dependence does not always indicate a common purpose.' (2003, p.76). The critics have placed great significance in the mythological link from Kenyon to the metaphysical cults.

The Kenyon connection was a key point for the critics, but even if we ignored the historical and theological evidence that denies this connection, it has been noted by DeArteaga and agreed within the Perriman Report that we should warn against the: 'genetic fallacy of rejecting an idea because of where it comes from rather than disproving the argument' (2003, p.76; 1992, p.246).

Bowman concluded emphatically 'Kenyon never ministered in metaphysical contexts, never modeled his ministry institution on metaphysical ones, and was never received by the metaphysical community. By contrast, all three of these things are true of Kenyon's connections with the evangelical faith-cure and early Pentecostal movements' (2001, pp.66,67). The evidence for Kenyon's teaching as being within Christian theology is clear and emphatic. Similarly, is the case for the 'Word of Faith' movement, the evidence is weighty because it comes from both academic and independent voices. These are not 'Word of Faith' advocates necessarily, these are independent appraisals offering balance and clear-sightedness which exposes the often-unbalanced critics.

In its important conclusion, the Perriman Report argues somewhat positively regarding the 'Word of Faith' movement, stating that there is enough common ground for 'rapprochement between the 'Word of Faith' movement and the more mainstream evangelical church' (2003, p.230). Rapprochement involves the resumption of relationships and cooperation. It is important to be aware that it is the critics mythology alone, which has been so potentially divisive to the relationships of believers. The conclusions of this significant and academic report are clearly at odds with the conclusions of the critics who have been led by the mythology of McConnell, Hannegraff, MacArthur, Peters and others.

Therefore, the proof is clear, the attacks against the 'Word of Faith' movement are out of balance with the leading and authoritative academic analysis. These definitive proofs provide us with substantial evidence which exposes McConnell, Hanegraaff, MacArthur, Peters and the other critics' mythology. Their conclusions are both historically and theologically erroneous and divisive. It is one thing to expose error and heresy justly and correctly when it truly exists, the Bible gives us a clear direction to: *'Preach the word; be instant in season, out of season; reprove, rebuke, exhort with all longsuffering and doctrine'* (2 Timothy 4:2). However, to make vigorous and unyielding accusations against the 'Word of Faith' movement, that are then exposed as errors by the most authoritative voices, reveals a remarkable irony alongside a serious abuse of position and trust. In addition, this shows a desire towards embracing dissension and a gross lack of wisdom. The Bible advises us about the type of wisdom that believers should employ: *'But the wisdom that is from above is first pure, then peaceable, gentle, and easy to be intreated, full of mercy and good fruits, without partiality, and without hypocrisy'* (James 3:17).

The critics have not demonstrated that they truly understood the wider influences of the movement that they were attempting to engage with. They had gathered together some of the more provocative statements of the movement, but they didn't grasp the foundational basis of the movement because their presuppositions were wrong. The erroneous claim of a metaphysical link for example, impacted on their ability to understand the truth of the movement. Also, a broader, less biased field of referencing would have helped. It has been observed by anthropologist Charles Kraft for example, that 'when a world view is supernaturalistic, it is common for people to regard material goods as signs of the blessing of God' (Kraft 1996, p.189).

This and similar observations of Pentecostal and Charismatic rooted believers, have been entirely overlooked by the critics. We will see later in this work that this view applies within both the Old and New Testaments. The 'Word of Faith' movement has also embraced a Biblical supernatural approach, all notions of prosperity should, therefore, have been understood as normative and entirely expected.

The Perriman Report

The Perriman Report, as mentioned previously, will be cited because it is the most significant research paper to date on the 'Word of Faith' movement. It was commissioned by the British Evangelical Alliance and reaches important conclusions for both the 'Word of Faith' movement and the critics. In its important conclusion, the Perriman Report argues relatively positively for the 'Word of Faith' movement. It states, shunning the 'cultic' accusations of the critics, that there is enough common ground for 'rapprochement between the 'Word of Faith' movement and the more mainstream evangelical church' (2003, p.230). It then goes on to suggest, '...that there is more to the teaching of Hagin and Copeland than is found in the one-sided analysis of their opponents' (2003, p.232).

Despite its non-cultic conclusion, the Perriman Report does suggest areas of concern where more thought is needed, and lessons can be learned.

Doubtless, this would have been observed for any movement that was put under such significant and wide-ranging scrutiny. The report offers an authoritative critique which addresses the imbalance and prejudices that have often hindered appraisals of the movement to date. It considers historical, religious, and cultural circumstances and in so doing contributes towards a context which has often been missing in the debate.

The conclusions of this significant and academic report are clearly at odds with the findings of the critics who have been led astray by their own mythology and often the heresy of cessationism.

Atonement theology

The Perriman Report suggests that the critics of the 'Word of Faith' movement claim that the movement 'diverges from sound doctrine at certain key points, most notably in its understanding of the atonement' (2003, p.14). However, neither the critics, nor the Perriman Report have offered what would constitute a sound understanding of the atonement. Therefore, we will explore this question and the 'Word of Faith' atonement theology will be examined by comparison to a leading recognized historical authority on the subject, Bishop Gustaf Aulén (1879-1978).

Aulén is known as one of the most influential contributors in the area of historical doctrines of the atonement. Through his well-respected book Christus Victor he established himself as one of the key contributors in the field. Aulén observed that throughout church history there have been three keyways of understanding the atonement. The point here is, at times we understand the same truth from different perspectives. The truth remains and is constant but the perspective changes, depending on our context. Bishop Gustaf Aulén observed this in his assessment of the atonement, his views are:

1) 'Classical' or 'Ransom' theory
2) 'Penal Substitution' or 'Satisfaction' doctrine
3) 'Protestant Orthodoxy' or 'Exchange' doctrine

He advocated a return to the 'classic' view, which he summarized as a Divine conflict and victory. In this view, 'Christ fights against and triumphs over the evil powers of the world, the 'tyrants' under which mankind is in bondage and suffering. In Christ, God reconciles the world to Himself. This view has often been adopted, to varying degrees, by the

'Word of Faith' movement. The movement, like most Christian movements to some degree, has been influenced by all three of the views cited above. The key point here is, this demonstrates how the critics have been wrong to accuse the 'Word of Faith' movement of heresy. In truth, much of the accusations are due to their narrow theological and historical scope of reference.

It will be shown that the movement has an atonement doctrine that is clearly within the parameters of historic Christian theology. This clearly exposes the conclusions of the critics as having been less than historically and theologically accurate. Hanegraaff cites the atonement as one of the essential issues for the unity of doctrine (1993, p.47). However, he offers no recognized definition for the atonement. Instead, he attacks the 'Word of Faith' movement for their atonement doctrine. Here lies a serious and exposing issue against the critics, the 'Word of Faith' movement's atonement doctrine, is recognizably orthodox. It seems that Hanegraaff, like McConnell, was either unaware of, or has simply overlooked the history of atonement doctrine within the church. Hanegraaff goes on to ironically quote Saint Augustine whose wise words should be taken on board by those who seek to offer critique: 'In essentials, unity; in nonessentials, liberty; and in all things, charity.' (1993, p47). Charity indeed!

The mythology in summary

I have listed the main points of influence on this work below, but this work is not limited to these points. We will uncover other related issues. We will expose the mythology of the leading critics of the 'Word of Faith' movement, who have claimed:

1) Kenyon was the father of the movement because of his influence over Hagin.
2) Kenyon had links to the metaphysical cults.
3) Therefore, the metaphysical cults influenced the 'Word of Faith' movement.
4) The 'Word of Faith' movement's atonement doctrine is cultic.
5) Word of Faith' theology is generally cultic.

Within this work, we will show clear historical and theological evidence to disprove the critics' claims.

It will be shown that:

1) Kenyon wasn't the movements father, but he remains an influential figure.
2) Kenyon didn't have links with metaphysical cults.
3) There are no metaphysical influences on the 'Word of Faith' movement.
4) The 'Word of Faith' movement's theology is not cultic.
5) Kenneth Hagin is the Father of the 'Word of Faith' movement.
6) The 'Word of Faith' atonement doctrine will be shown to be within the parameters of historical and theological orthodoxy.
7) The 'Word of Faith' movement's roots can be traced back to the Pentecostal and Charismatic church.
8) The 'Word of Faith' movement employs a Biblical theology.
9) McConnell and the subsequent critics have created a mythology to attack the 'Word of Faith' movement.
10) The critics of the 'Word of Faith' movement have facilitated
11) liberalism.
12) The 'Word of Faith' critics have been divisive against the Christian church.
13) The 'Word of Faith' movement has been a significant worldwide move of God.

Chapter 2
Some of the people involved

Daniel McConnell

McConnell is referenced in this work because it was, he, who created the mythology that most other critics have subsequently followed. The mythology claims that the 'Word of Faith' movement offers 'a different Gospel,' because of its:

1) Historical origins.
2) Heretical doctrines.
3) Cultic practices (McConnell p.183).

McConnell and the many other critics who followed his claims have created a mythology. We can prove that a mythology exists for the following reasons:

1) The historical evidence doesn't support their claims.
2) The theological evidence doesn't support their claims.
3) The conclusions are demonstratively wrong.

Therefore, as a result of the above, the attempts by the critics to understand the 'Word of Faith' movement have been cynical and wrong. It will be shown with expert theological and historical evidence that their analysis has been based on errors and they have created a divisive and erroneous mythology.

McConnell's critique was made during his Master's degree at Oral Roberts University in 1982 under the heading, 'The Kenyon Connection: A Theological and Historical Analysis of the Cultic Origins of the Faith Movement.' It was subsequently published in 1988 under the title 'A Different Gospel.' In McConnell's mythology, 'The Kenyon Connection,' is the link between metaphysical cults and the 'Word of Faith' movement. The mythology he invented suggests that the metaphysical cults significantly impacted E. W. Kenyon. He then develops the myth that Kenneth Hagin's plagiarizing of Kenyon, subsequently allowed the metaphysical cults to influence the 'Word of Faith' movement. McConnell claims that Kenyon is the 'Father' of the 'Word of Faith' movement because of his influence through Hagin (1995, pp.29-54).

This mythology was controversial when first introduced but has become the mythology of choice for critics of the movement, to the degree that, it is often taken for granted. Bowler, for example, published by Oxford University Press, promotes the mythology and considers, 'E. W. Kenyon the theological architect' of the 'Word of Faith' movement (Bowler 2013, p.250). The critics, often caring little for accuracy or truth, simply perpetuate the mythology of the link to the metaphysical cults. Within this work we will demonstrate why this is clearly indefensible. The critics arguments are often developed upon a series of myths and presuppositions. Sadly, the victims, are often those who are sincerely seeking the hope of the Gospel and a Biblical foundation for their lives.

The extent of McConnell's flawed arguments are such, that his accusations have at times fueled significant doubt and created many divisions within the church. The division reached a peak at the turn of the century when countless churches were denouncing any charismatic manifestations. Someone might laugh, someone else might get suspicious and soon enough another church would split. Behind it all were the accusations and mythology of the cessationists.

McConnell's claims are at times, nothing short of bizarre, for example he suggests that, 'The Faith theology is based on Cultic presuppositions' (1995, p.187). He goes on to call his mythology an 'appeal to the pastors and lay people of the faith movement' to recognize the following: (1) The cultic historical origins of their movement; (2) The degree to which these origins have influenced their doctrines and practices; and (3) The need to recant these cultic doctrines and practices and reconstruct their theology upon a more solid biblical foundation (1995, p.187). In other words, he has based his denouncing of the faith movement to a mythological link that he had invented between Kenyon and the metaphysical cults. McConnell himself claims that Kenyon's theological links to metaphysics are 'well disguised' (1988, p.50). In other words, by his own admission, the obvious facts don't truly match with his position but nevertheless, he jumbles a biased and selective history with an equally selectively narrow theology, to create a mythology. He then uses that to accuse the 'Word of Faith' movement of being 'cultic in historical origin' (1995, p.50). It will be shown that McConnell's mythology has had to ignore readily available facts that emphatically separate Kenyon from the metaphysical cults.

We will also show that there was no disguise, or anything cultic, but rather an accepted Christian belief system based on Biblical Christianity. Like many new movements within church history, the 'Word of Faith' movement has introduced theological truths from a fresh perspective. The Reformation did the same with subjects such as grace, faith and salvation. At times, these teachings have been misrepresented by critics and misunderstood. The 'Word of Faith' movement has not set out to create full theological appraisals of Christian doctrines, rather it has offered a theology 'from below.' It has been concerned with understanding the Biblical texts from a practical empirical perspective. The movement originates not in the seats of theological thought in Universities but in the practical needs of people, often in difficult circumstances, who recognize that they need salvation for their lives. People who need answers to the issues of life, who need the true Gospel of Jesus Christ as revealed in the Bible. The critics have failed to recognize this practical paradigm.

The movement has been clear in what it has stood for, for example, Kenyon himself repeatedly criticizes the metaphysical cults in the strongest and clearly Biblical terms possible. Here's one very clear example of what Kenyon teaches: 'One of them calls Him (Jesus) "the way shower." He is not the way shower, HE IS THE WAY! Their (Metaphysical cults) faith in Jesus and faith in God is, after all, faith in themselves, and what they inherently have within themselves' (1942, pp.17-18).

Kenyon's position was not based in his own mental assent, which is the metaphysical cults' position, but rather on his faith in God. He makes this distinction repeatedly very clear: 'It is not mental as Christian Science and other metaphysical teachers claim' (Kenyon 1943, p.90). With such a clear and repeated differentiation from Kenyon's own teaching towards the metaphysical cults, it is difficult to understand how the critics could possibly defend their claims. McConnell's position demands firstly, that we ignore the proof of Kenyon's own repeated teachings regarding metaphysics. He then wants his audience to explore myth and pursue what he classifies as, 'well disguised' doctrines. To embrace McConnell's critical mythology, it would take a significant commitment to refuse to accept large portions of historical and theological evidence. This is what the critics, often called "Heresy hunters' have committed themselves to doing.

McConnell and the many who have followed his arguments have attacked the 'Word of Faith' atonement doctrine as if it was only the 'Word of Faith' movement who have adopted certain theological points. McConnell doesn't cite anyone else as believing anything like the 'Word of Faith' movement, his critique isolates the movement. For the uninformed observer, this can make it appear that 'Word of Faith' theology is entirely different to other recognized Christian beliefs. This study will show that the 'Word of Faith' movement's atonement theology for example, is shared by many and that it is certainly not as McConnell suggests, a 'House of cards' (1995, p127). McConnell seemed to be unaware of the historical authenticity of the atonement theology that Kenyon often referenced. Kenyon often used the 'classic' atonement view. This view emerged with Christianity itself and was popularized by Origen, it remained dominant for the first thousand years of the Christian church (1965, pp.49,158).

Hank Hanegraaff

Hanegraaff, like most of the critics, has followed McConnell's mythology and claims, 'The Faith movement' has systematically subverted the very essence of Christianity so as to present us with a counterfeit Christ and a counterfeit Christianity. Therefore, standing against the theology of the 'Word of Faith' movement does not divide; rather, it unites believers' (1993, p.48). The Perriman Report has taken care to refuse to agree with Hanegraaff repeatedly, commenting on one occasion that his conclusion of 'blasphemy' was so inappropriate, it was classified as nothing more than an 'outraged accusation' (2003, p.109).

Hanegraaff is prone to polarized claims which are largely based on historical and theological inaccuracies, these will be highlighted within this work. Often, the critics use inappropriate and inaccurate illustrations to dramatize their points, Hanegraaff for example, justifies his harshness against the faith teachers by comparing himself to the Apostle Paul who had to similarly be harsh with Elymas in Acts 13 (1993, p79). However, on reading about Elymas we find how inappropriate, harsh, and somewhat ironic Hanegraaff's critique truly is: *'But Elymas the sorcerer (for so is his name by interpretation) withstood them, seeking to turn away the deputy from the faith'* (Acts 13:8). In other words, Hanegraaff has been so biased against the movement that he compares the 'Word of Faith' people to a sorcerer! That is an outrageous comparison to make. We should also further consider that Hanegraaff, the self-styled 'Bible Answer Man,' fails to recognize that the text points to Elymas' desire to turn people away from the faith! Elymas therefore, is according to the Bible, diametrically opposite to the 'Word of Faith' movement. Elymas was against *'the faith!'* Nevertheless, Hanegraaff seems so set on his attack, he offers it regardless of historical facts or a clear recognizable Biblical hermeneutic. This is a pattern that he and the other critics use repeatedly. It seems that they presume to throw so much mythological mud, that surely some is bound to stick.

Hanegraaff's 1993 critique of the 'Word of Faith' movement 'Christianity in Crisis,' begins with a characterization of the 'Word of Faith' movement's most influential leaders (1993, pp.29-41). However, the Perriman Report has observed in its challenge to those outside of the 'Word of Faith' movement that, 'caricatures help to highlight excess and hypocrisy, but they are an indiscriminate instrument of polemic' (2003, p.231-4). In other words, the danger of creating caricatures is that it causes a generalization to take place and for the 'Word of Faith' movement, these generalizations fail to engage in the complexity of the fusion of doctrines that exist. Within this work, for example, a complicated fusion of doctrines will be shown to exist in the atonement. Any caricature of the 'Word of Faith' movement's atonement doctrine, as has been shown, fails to distinguish these complexities and reduces itself to the compartmentalization often found in extreme critical perspectives. According to the Perriman Report, some of the critics of the 'Word of Faith' movement have adopted polarized positions, which in turn have led to extreme classifications of the movement as 'cultic' (2003, p.15). DeArteaga's response to Hanegraaff's polarized 'Christianity in Crisis' book, is worth repeating. He suggests that, 'behind its numerous citations and quotations lays a profound methodological error – the assumption that listing the worst errors of a movement is a truthful representation of that movement' (1992, p.269). Clearly, DeArteaga has made a useful and prudent observation.

Hanegraaff is one in a long line of critics to use McConnell's radical mythology. His arguments will be shown to lack both theological accuracy and an appreciation of historical Christian views. He repeatedly demonstrated a blinding critical position regarding the 'Word of Faith' movement and often reached nothing short of extremely unfair conclusions. For example, he claims that Kenneth Copeland Ministries bears all the marks of a 'cult' because it has: A) A formalized hierarchical structure B)

A centralized organizational facility C) A publishing arm D) Distribution (1993, p45). It's impossible to understand how a 'cult' designation could be drawn from having what can be deemed as perfectly normal facilities for Christian ministry. The Billy Graham Evangelistic Association has the same facilities. Indeed, the same facilities could be found within The Christian Research Institute that Hanegraaff led at the time of publishing his attack. It seems as if the critics employ an energetic liberty to throw all manner of accusations against the 'Word of Faith' movement regardless to substance or factual realities.

Perhaps the most serious issue regarding Hanegraaff is that he calls the 'Word of Faith' doctrine reprehensible (1993, p164) for their atonement doctrines. In this, Hanegraaff exposes his theological weaknesses the most. A study of the history of the atonement doctrine within the recognized worldwide church, reveals that the atonement doctrine of the 'Word of Faith' movement is a mix of that which is historically and theologically orthodox. Hanegraaff doesn't offer an assessment of what the church has believed regarding the atonement, but we will within this work. This will show that the 'Word of Faith' position has adopted clearly recognizable views, shared at least in part, by many Christians outside the 'Word of Faith' movement and these are theologically orthodox. Perhaps, what is truly reprehensible is the lack of balanced research behind Hanegraaff's attacks and the thin veneer of academia behind his manipulative and extensive use of references.

Like McConnell, Hanegraaff used mythology and characterization to a significant degree in his criticism of the 'Word of Faith' movement. His characterization of the whole movement for example, as being a 'kingdom of the cults,' typifies this cynical approach (1993, p71). Within this examination of the 'Word of Faith' movement, it will be shown that Hanegraaff and McConnell, like the subsequent critics, have jointly shared erroneous and divisive arguments. What is also concerning is that Hanegraaff indulges in his own mythology and justifies his harshness by comparing himself to Biblical prophets of old (1993, p.79). So not only does he paint a negative mythology of the 'Word of Faith' movement but he also creates a positive mythology of himself as both the 'Bible Answer Man' and profit of God. His polarizations are excessive and extreme.

Having joined the Eastern Orthodox church, Hanegraaff's presuppositions and notions of orthodox doctrines, might be very different from what some of his 'Christianity in Crisis' audience might have presumed? It is also interesting to note that when Hanegraaff joined the Eastern Orthodox church, those 'Word of Faith' ministries which had been unfairly and harshly criticized by him, remained silent against perhaps the loudest of their accusers.

The result of Hanegraaff's efforts can be seen in the existence of ongoing divisions within the church, church splits, and significant confusion for some believers. Some probably well-intentioned but ill-informed believers have adopted Hanegraaff's views and at times have confronted 'Word of Faith' believers with a surprising level of aggression. It seems that Hanegraaff's extreme denouncing of the movement has charged their instincts to protect the church they love. The irony is, that the church they love and its Biblical truth, are precisely what the 'Word of Faith' movement is defending.

Justin Peters

An example of one of the most recent critics peddling the critical mythology is Justin Peters. In his seminar 'A Call for Discernment,' Peters promotes the mythology that the movement's origins are in New Thought metaphysics from the late 19th and early 20th centuries. Peters describes himself on his own website in the following way, "An evangelist with two earned seminary degrees, known by many around the world, and widely regarded to be the foremost authority on Word-Faith" [Peters 2019]. He makes his substantial claims regarding his authoritative position, despite his extremely bizarre past. He claims that he has been doing the same seminars on the 'Word of Faith' movement since 2004. It's interesting that he hasn't changed the seminars over the years, as by his own dramatic admission, he was not even converted until 2011. Therefore, as a non-Christian from 2004 to part way through 2011, he travelled around the world criticizing Christian ministers of the 'Word of Faith' movement whilst pretending to be a Christian minister! He partially justifies that position by explaining that despite not being a Christian he was nevertheless preaching truth [Peters 2019]. The utter implausibility of that theory seems to be entirely lost to him but the Bible is very clear, *'If we say that we have fellowship with him, and walk in darkness, we lie, and do not the truth'* (1 John 1:6). Given Peters' admission, we might hope that in future years, he might make further changes and perhaps turn from peddling the old mythology regarding the 'Word of Faith' movement.

The strap-line for his ministry comes from Romans 11:36, *'For from him and through him and for him are all things. To him be the glory forever! Amen.'* It seems that for Peters not everyone can give glory to God for all things, some things such as private airplanes, are just too much for God. Peters' ministry website peddles the critical mythology, sells videos and offers lectures against the 'Word of Faith' movement. His line of critique presents the usual moribund theology, history and characterizations enroute to creating mythology. Sadly, for some lacking in discernment, these extreme positions might appear to be plausible on the surface. The Bible teaches us: *'Now I urge you, brethren, note those who cause divisions and offenses, contrary to the doctrine which you learned, and avoid them'* (Romans 16:17).

Sadly, Peters, like many of the critics not only *'Cause divisions'* but they are also cessationists. Cessationists refuse to believe large portions of the Bible and they believe instead that spiritual gifts such as speaking in tongues, prophecy and healing, ceased with the apostolic age. From this position of denial and doubt, the Biblical emphasis of the 'Word of Faith' movement has become the target of their heresy.

Peters, in what has become a common trend of the critics, continues contributing to the mythology by outrageously inventing imaginary accusations against the 'Word of Faith' movement. In one Youtube video for example, Peters shows a clip of Kenneth Copeland and Jesse Duplantis in conversation. Jesse Duplantis is talking about sitting in his private plane, when the Lord spoke to him about his faith stagnating. He responded by unbuckling his seatbelt, standing up and then praying to God. In response, Kenneth Copeland observed that, "You couldn't have done that on an airliner." Any right-thinking person would agree, if you stand up on an airliner, lift your hands and pray out loud, you might even create a panic situation. Copeland then explains that someone might ask, "What the Hell's he think he's doing?" Copeland was rightly explaining the limitations and difficulty of commercial airline travel in comparison to private. Copeland went on to explain that years ago, when Oral Roberts used to fly airlines, people were coming up to Roberts to talk and ask for prayer. In the end, it became difficult to travel as a famous person. He then explains that in general, airline travel today has become even worse. Many of us would agree, having experienced drunks on planes, rude people and the uncomfortable limitations of space. For people traveling a lot and doing the most important work on planet Earth, spreading the Gospel of Jesus Christ, ease of transportation is a blessing of God. In 3 John 2 for example, we read, *'Beloved, I wish above all things that thou mayest prosper and be in health, even as thy soul prospereth.'* When the New Testament says *'that thou mayest prosper,'* this word only appears in the following two other places: In Romans 1:10 it means, *'to have a prosperous journey'* and in 1 Corinthians 16:2 it means, *'hath prospered.'* In 3 John 2, it conveys a meaning of being led in a good way; to prosper one's journey. This includes an understanding to make prosperous in all ways and as Barnes has noted: 'would apply here to any plan or purpose entertained. It would include success in business, happiness in domestic relations, or prosperity in any of the engagements and transactions in which a Christian might lawfully engage. It shows that it is right to wish that our friends may have success in the works of their hands and their plans of life' (Biblehubcom: 2019). Obviously, right thinking people ought to be pleased when a minister can travel with prosperity by a private plane rather than a far more difficult commercial airline. Anyone who is wanting to impose a harsher and less prosperous journey on believers, is diametrically opposed to the Bible's clear and stated position.

In the video clip, Jesse Duplantis then goes on to explain to Kenneth Copeland that he showed one of his flying schedules to a Delta Airlines Captain who confirmed that Jesse Duplantis couldn't fly such a busy schedule with them. The conversation was pointing out the many advantages of private jet travel, as opposed to commercial jet travel.

Peters then goes into details of how he once used a Kenneth Copeland employee to gain entrance into Copeland's private jet. He then makes the false claim that Copeland told Duplantis in the video clip shown that: "You notice that Kenneth Copeland told Jesse that you couldn't talk to God on a commercial airline" (Youtubecom: 2019). This is blatant, unashamed, and emphatic myth creation in action. Copeland simply didn't say that! Peters then repeats what he has made up and attributes it again to Copeland. In this short clip alone, he made the claim three times, that Copeland has told Jesse Duplantis "You can't talk to God on a commercial airline." Peters continues creating his mythology by saying: "All the prayers that I've prayed, and probably you have prayed on an airliner, sitting in a coach seat, you know, in the back of the plane, God doesn't hear those prayers. So, you have to be in a private jet for God to hear you." Peters infers that these words belong to Kenneth Copeland and Jesse Duplantis, but they didn't say anything like this on the video. They didn't say that a person is unable to pray on a commercial airliner and neither did they say that you needed to be in a private jet to pray. Peters has simply made the entire narrative up. He has the effrontery to then attribute these words to Copeland and Duplantis, when they are his words. The deception is bold and arrogant showing total disregard to the truth or the integrity of the words of Copeland and Duplantis.

He then concludes, without any hint of irony or self-awareness, with these words: "This speaks to the absolute moral and theological bankruptcy of these charlatans that you see on Christian television, it is just unbelievable." When he says, "it is just unbelievable" on this point, I think we can find common ground and agree. Anyone watching the clip can witness that Kenneth Copeland and Jesse Duplantis don't say what Peters claims they say. Peters' position is clearly unbelievable given the video evidence.

The concern is that that he is actively promoting this mythology and clearly leading people astray from truth and reality. Peters, like most of the critics, doesn't seem to be concerned at all about the accuracy of his words, integrity, or truth. Another irony exists in that the ones who have been shouting the loudest that the 'Word of Faith' movement lacks theological truth and morality, are upon examination, well qualified to have these charges made of them. Shakespeare's Hamlet comes to mind, in that the mythology makers "doth protest too much." This then begs the question, why? In Peters' case, he admits in the video clip that he has a personal interest in aircraft, possibly the inaccurate and extreme position adopted by Peters, pertains more to his deep unquenched personal desires?

The mythology pushers have a common strategy of negativity that is aimed at undermining faith and belief within the church. This is what Peters and the other mythology pushers do, they take something and push it to an extreme. Peters is so critical, he doesn't even think that he personally was a believer, for the first 7 years of his own ministry.

Robert Bowman

Robert Bowman is a theologian referenced in part because his conclusion was deemed to be the most important academic assessment available by the Perriman Report and 'probably the most balanced and judicious analysis of the movement to date' (2003, p.14). However, Bowman is not overly favorable to the 'Word of Faith' movement. It is therefore very interesting to note that in his conclusion, he went against the leader of the organization that he was working for at The Christian Research Institute. The leader of the Institute happened to be Hank Hanegraaff, one of the chief critics and proponents of the mythology against the 'Word of Faith' movement. Bowman's conclusion was striking because of this context and whilst he highlighted certain areas that he felt needed to be addressed within the movement, he demonstrated a more academic methodology of appraisal.

This led to a different conclusion than critics such as Hanegraaff and McConnell, that the 'Word of Faith' movement was not cultic. Similarly, to the Perriman Report, Robert Bowman concluded that the 'Word of Faith' movement's roots are to be found within Pentecostalism rather than the metaphysical cults (2001, p.12). This is a very important conclusion, by the most judicious and academic observers, as it emphatically exposes the errors of the mythology. Further, Bowman advises that the movement ought not to be described as cultic (2001, p.228). Therefore, the attacks against the 'Word of Faith' movement can be viewed as being clearly out of balance with the leading and authoritative, independent, academic analysis.

E. W. Kenyon

Kenyon was converted at a Methodist service at age seventeen, and two years later he was a licensed Methodist Pastor in New York (McIntyre 1997, p.3). However, it wasn't long before he entered a difficult period where he left the ministry to pursue training as an actor. Towards this end, Kenyon entered the 'Emerson College of Oratory' in 1892, but on a visit to A. J. Gordon's famous evangelical Baptist Church in Boston, he rededicated his life to Christian service. Within two years Kenyon was a Pastor within the Free Will Baptist denomination. It is obvious to say but worth noting, to help dispel the metaphysical link, that this Christian denomination had no connection with the metaphysical cults. The metaphysical link is of key importance to the mythology of the critics and they have ignored the implications of Kenyon's clearly orthodox position with the Baptist denomination.

The Free Will Baptists had been heavily influenced by the Holiness revivals of the 1890's which emphasized a dependence of the Bible and at times miraculous healings. In particular, McIntyre has noted that Kenyon was influenced by the Faith-Cure Christian evangelical movement, which was well respected amongst the Charismatic and Pentecostal Christian communities (1997, p.226). Soon Kenyon was in high demand as a public preacher and Bible teacher, and in response to repeated requests (2003, p.70) for him to run a Bible study, in 1900 he established the Bethel Bible Institute in Spencer, Massachusetts. For the next 23 years Kenyon was the principal of the Bethel Bible College, however, in 1923 he left citing funding issues and began working as an interdenominational itinerant evangelist alongside renowned Pentecostal leaders, such as Aimee Semple McPherson, and F. F. Bosworth. Kenyon worked with, and was associated with, well known Pentecostal leaders. These people, like Kenyon himself, were not on the edge of metaphysics but soundly in Biblical Christian beliefs. Their emphasis was on the Bible, on healing through the atonement, on promoting the Gospel of Jesus Christ.

In 1931 Kenyon moved to Seattle where he founded the New Covenant Baptist Church. It was during this period that he wrote many of his most famous books and worked as a local Pastor until his death in 1948. His influence was significant during his lifetime, and there was no evidence of him being connected to the metaphysical cults until McConnell's mythology was offered in 1982. By this time, the 'Word of Faith' movement was well established, and Hagin was regarded as the movements clear 'Father.' As noted by Bowman earlier, McConnell's attempt to link Kenyon to the metaphysical cults and being the movement's 'Father' was shocking, but it gained momentum. Bowman correctly asserts that McConnell and the mythology makers are wrong to link Kenyon to the metaphysical cults. He writes, 'Kenyon assumed the absolute reliability of the Bible and interpreted it without recourse to esoteric, metaphysical explanations. He therefore self-consciously rejected the metaphysical cults on doctrinal grounds' (2001, p.54).

According to McConnell, Hagin took over the mantle of what has come to be known as, 'Word of Faith' teachings by reading Kenyon's published material (1988, p.7). What McConnell has overlooked is the vast amount of work that Hagin developed that was not influenced by Kenyon. Hagin would use Kenyon's material among others, and he clearly respected Kenyon, but McConnell has exaggerated the influence, to establish a mythological cultic link.

Kenneth E. Hagin

The leading representative and the 'Father' of the 'Word of Faith' movement was Kenneth Hagin (1917-2003). Kenneth E. Hagin is often recognized as the founder of the 'Word of Faith' movement. Hagin's fresh perspective on faith is clear from the title of one of his most popular books, which suggests that when faith is employed, 'You Can Have What You Say' (2003, p.3). His ministry has been succeeded by his son Kenneth Hagin Jr., but as the Perriman Report has noted, the true successor to Hagin has been his former student Kenneth Copeland (Perriman 2003, p.4).

Hagin was born in McKinney, Texas, and according to his testimony, he was born with a deformed heart and with an incurable blood disease. He was not expected to live long, and by the age of 15 he was paralyzed and bedridden. On August 8, 1934, he says he was raised from his deathbed by a revelation of faith in God's Word after reading Mark 11:22-23. The Bible verses from Mark 11:22-24 came to define and summarize Hagin's ministry, they read: *'And Jesus answering saith unto them, Have faith in God. 23 For verily I say unto you, That whosoever shall say unto this mountain, Be thou removed, and be thou cast into the sea; and shall not doubt in his heart, but shall believe that those things which he saith shall come to pass; he shall have whatsoever he saith. 24 Therefore I say unto you, What things soever ye desire, when ye pray, believe that ye receive them, and ye shall have them.'*

Hagin started his preaching ministry as a young man in 1936. He Pastored several churches before his last pastorate in Van, Texas. From that time onwards he began his itinerant traveling ministry. Hagin started as a Bible teacher and evangelist in 1949 and joined the Voice of Healing Revival in the U.S. ministering alongside people such as Oral Roberts, Gordon Lindsay, and T. L. Osborn. In 1963 the Kenneth E. Hagin Evangelistic Association (now Kenneth Hagin Ministries) was founded and by 1966 the ministry offices were moved from Garland, Texas, to Tulsa, Oklahoma. That same year also saw the start of his radio ministry, and he was ordained by The North Texas District Council of the Assemblies of God as a minister in 1967.

In 1974, Hagin founded the most extensive single 'Word of Faith' Training College in Broken Arrow, Oklahoma. The Rhema Bible Training College has training centers in fourteen different countries and has over 40,000 alumni. Hagin has also founded one of the 'Word of Faith' movements leading publishing houses Faith Library Publications.

It was in 1979 that Buddy Harrison, Hagin's son-in-law, alongside other 'Word of Faith' ministers, founded the International Convention of Faith Ministries (ICFM). The ICFM with the initiative of Buddy Harrison, who was also the owner of the highly influential Harrison House Publishers, flourished as the main hub for the movement's ministers. This ministerial association is now based in Arlington, Texas and along with the Rhema Ministerial Association International (RMAI) which was formed in 1985, continues to provide the 'Word of Faith's main network hub. In the ICFM, Hagin was the senior founding minister and as this was the most prominent 'Word of Faith' ministerial network, acknowledging Hagin as the movements 'Father' is a straightforward conclusion to draw. It is also worth noting that in 1978 Jim and Kathleen Kaseman founded the first Association of Faith Churches and Ministers (AFCM), many others have followed, but the ICFM and RMAI continue to lead the way.

In 1979, Hagin also founded the Prayer and Healing Center as provision for the sick to come and 'have the opportunity to build their faith.' The Healing School continues to be held free of charge twice a day on the RHEMA campus. Hagin has extended his influence through publishing a magazine entitled, 'The Word of Faith,' which has 600,000 monthly subscribers.

One of Hagin's many teachings which are shared within the 'Word of Faith' movement is that words spoken in faith, will result in a person getting what they say. Hagin explained that there were four steps to receiving from God: (1) Say it, (2) Do it, (3) Receive it, and (4) Tell it. He explains that 'If you talk about your trials, your difficulties, your lack of faith, your lack of money your faith will shrivel and dry up' (1979, pp.3-8). Some people criticize Hagin for what to some, might seem to be, a strong stance in this area. However, clearly Hagin's position is developed in the main, from the Bible itself. Jesus' teaching in Mark 11 verses 22-24 for example: *'So Jesus answered and said to them, "Have faith in God. For assuredly, I say to you, whoever says to this mountain, 'Be removed and be cast into the sea,' and does not doubt in his heart, but believes that those things he says will be done, he will have whatever he says. Therefore I say to you, whatever things you ask when you pray, believe that you receive them, and you will have them.'* Here we can see that Hagin is explaining directly from Jesus' teaching, he is being faithful to the text rather than reducing the text to something more palatable to human experience. This is something that the critics, in the main, from the constraints of western theological anti-supernaturalism, have been unable to grasp. The possibility that the 'Word of Faith' movement is founded on Biblical promises based on Jesus' words, is an anathema to most Enlightenment based critics. Or to put it another way, the critics haven't attempted to explain, why they presume that Jesus' words are not applicable today.

The 'Word of Faith' movement has responded to Jesus' words by daring to believe them. Again, we can go to Jesus' words directly, to see the validity in this position: *'And whatever things you ask in prayer, believing, you will receive'* (Matthew 21:22). No amount of Biblical contextualization, higher or lower criticism, can take away the stark promise of Jesus' words. The Greek text is clear enough in all the versions available, the question for a follower of Jesus is therefore, will they ask in prayer and believe? This has been an emphasis of the 'Word of Faith' movement that the critics have overlooked, they haven't been able to directly answer the Biblical text itself. Usually, the critics simply repeatedly deny the potent words of Jesus Christ through their own doctrine of cessationism.

The integrity of the 'Word of Faith' movement has been shown in its willingness to believe the Bible. This simplicity of belief ought not to be overlooked or underestimated, it is in the final analysis an act of profound obedience.

Kenneth Copeland

We will now look at the ministry of Kenneth Copeland who is regarded by many as the leading figure within the current 'Word of Faith' movement. Following 'Daddy' Hagin's ministry, Copeland has been the most influential and lasting voice within the 'Word of Faith' movement. We will explore Copeland's views on prosperity and find that he offers a distinctive and thorough teaching with a strong Biblical emphasis.

The 'Word of Faith' critics often accuse the movement of having an overemphasis on prosperity. However, the Bible has a lot to say about prosperity, and Kenneth Copeland has helped to provide the 'Word of Faith' movement, and many others, with a fresh insight into Biblical prosperity. Copeland decided at the start of his ministry not to attempt to raise money through pleading for financial support as some were doing. Instead, he has cited going to God directly in prayer for wisdom and direction. His ministry gives people an opportunity to support via monthly partnerships and the daily television broadcast has a weekly Friday offering slot. Copeland has amassed significant wealth, a large portion of which, has come from having discovered significant reserves of natural gas on his property.

In response to his critics, Copeland teaches that he has chosen to walk in love, he explains, 'I love them because that's what Jesus told us to do (2011, p.304). This is foundational to Copeland's ministry and he quotes Jesus' words as His foundation: *'But I say to you who hear: Love your enemies, do good to those who hate you, bless those who curse you, and pray for those who spitefully use you'* (Luke 6:27,28). He has been attacked by the critics perhaps more than any other modern preacher. He was significantly influenced by Kenneth Hagin, who also had a strong emphasis on love and like Copeland, he has described the Christian life as the 'Love walk' (2005, p.68) (2011, p.293).

In the following chapter, we will explore the important ministry of the 'Word of Faith' movement's most senior minister, Kenneth Copeland.

Chapter 3

The ministry of Kenneth Copeland

Introduction

Within this chapter, we will explore the leading 'Word of Faith' exponent Kenneth Copeland. We will look at one of his most prominent teachings which has been classified both positively, and negatively by some, that of 'prosperity.' This will be based on information gathered through modern and historical Christian writings.

Copeland and other ministries from the 'Word of Faith' movement are sometimes confused by the critics with other satellite broadcasting ministries. For the critics, often anyone talking about 'prosperity' is classified as being part of the 'Word of Faith movement. However, the 'Word of Faith' movement has largely taken Copeland's lead, he writes: 'We declared that we would never ask any man for anything including money and places to minister. We pledged ourselves and this ministry to Romans 13:8, that we would never borrow one cent. We would tell our needs only to God and expect what He was teaching us to produce. Little did we know then what a blessing these standards would be' (1974, p.7).

In summary, many 'Word of Faith' ministries follow Copeland's guidance. Here we have listed his standards in point form:

1) Don't ask people for money
2) Don't ask people for places to minister
3) To walk in love (Romans 13:8)
4) Don't borrow money

5) Tell God your needs
6) Expect results from God's teaching
7) Live in the blessing of God

It is worth noting that Copeland, like most of the 'Word of Faith' movement, has showed a high level of integrity in adhering to these points. His debt free multi-million-dollar annual budgets, ought to cause people to seriously consider the points that he wrote about in his 1974 book cited above.

Copeland's spiritual father Hagin, wrote a well-balanced book on prosperity named, 'The Midas Touch.' In this work, Hagin described the issues at hand: 'There are those in the ditch on one side of the road who teach that Jesus lived in abject poverty, that money is evil, and that biblical prosperity has nothing at all to do with material things. And in the other ditch, there are people who are preaching that getting rich is the main focus of faith, that God's main concern is your material well-being, and that money is the true measure of spirituality. Where is the truth? It's found far away from both extremes, on much higher ground' (2000, p11).

Hagin, like Copeland, has stressed the that giving is one of the fruits of Biblical prosperity, he quotes John Wesley who also emphasized giving, 'Make all you can; save all you can; and give all you can' (1985, p.165).

Biblical prosperity

The foundation of prosperity for Copeland is seen within the Old Testament. In the book of Deuteronomy, Copeland explains that we can 'see the predominant rule to remember in living a prosperous life: *"But thou shalt remember the Lord thy God: for it is he that giveth thee the power to get wealth, that he may establish his covenant which he swore unto thy fathers, as it is this day"'* (Deuteronomy 8:17-18). Copeland goes on to highlight 'The predominant rule: God gives the power to get wealth. Why? To establish His covenant' (1974, p.35). He continues, in assessing Deuteronomy 28, where 'we see the blessings that come from obeying the Word of God. For instance, verses 11-12 state, *"And the Lord shall make thee plenteous in goods, in the fruit of thy body, and in the fruit of thy cattle, and in the fruit of thy ground, in the land which the Lord swore unto thy fathers to give thee. The Lord shall open unto thee his good treasure."* You see, God blessed Abraham and his descendants with prosperity because He swore it in the covenant. Praise God!' (1974, p.41).

For Copeland, the Babylonian system of the world is a debt system, which has entrapped most people. In the area of finances, he has demonstrated a different and Biblical path, he explains, 'How do you operate in financial situations without subordinating yourself to the world's system? What is the key that opens the channel in these things? It is available to us, but instead, all we have known is borrow, borrow, borrow! The Bible says if you will meditate in the Word of God day and night, you will have good success and deal wisely in your affairs. *The Word of God is the key'* (1974, p.91). The answer for Copeland is in the Biblical promise and direction that it offers believers. He has not merely theorized this as an option, but he has demonstrated it in his life. Clearly, he has shown a remarkable level of commitment and integrity to his beliefs and they have been validated empirically.

Many Christians, when they hear about prosperity, tend to recoil from it. Certain scriptures seem to enter their thinking such as Mark 10:25, which reads: *'It is easier for a camel to go through the eye of a needle than for a rich man to enter the kingdom of God.'* Their reaction is often due to either, a lack of Biblical knowledge themselves, or the influence of the critics such as Hanegraaff who have often failed to recognize the context of the verse (1993, p.206). This well-known and often quoted verse is in truth and context, a testimony to God's prosperity. Let's look at what the following two verses say to gain a context: *'And they were greatly astonished, saying among themselves, "Who then can be saved?" 27 But Jesus looked at them and said, "With men it is impossible, but not with God; for with God all things are possible."'* The disciples' question betrays the fact that within the first century, a rich man was regarded as being blessed by God. That's precisely why the disciples *'were greatly astonished!'* This also explains why they subsequently asked: *"Who then can be saved?"* The critics miss this central point entirely. If the rich man couldn't be saved and he was obviously blessed by God, what hope is there for the rest? The lack of ability to see this scripture in context, demonstrates clearly again, the compromised position of the 'Word of Faith' critics.

Some critics might quote the following scripture out of context: *'But godliness with contentment is great gain. 7 For we brought nothing into this world, and it is certain we can carry nothing out. 8 And having food and raiment let us be therewith content. 9 But they that will be rich fall into temptation and a snare, and into many foolish and hurtful lusts, which drown men in destruction and perdition. 10 For the love of money is the root of all evil: which while some coveted after, they have erred from the faith, and pierced themselves through with many sorrows. 11 But thou, O man of God, flee these things; and follow after righteousness, godliness, faith, love, patience, meekness'* (1 Timothy 6:6-11). This portion of scripture is about balance and wisdom but has at times been used by some prosperity critics to claim that, *'money is the root of all evil.'* However, the truth is that this scripture must be read in context, therefore, we can see that in verse 10 it teaches, *'for the love of money is the root of all evil.'* It's the *'love of money'* that's the issue. Prosperity doubters often take these verses out of context and use them to an exaggerated negative emphasis. To highlight this point, let's employ more context and look to the previous chapter of the same book. Here we can see the following two verses 17 and 18: *'Let the elders that rule well be counted worthy of double honour, especially they who labour in the word and doctrine. 18 For the scripture saith, thou shalt not muzzle the ox that treadeth out the corn. And, The labourer is worthy of his reward.'* The Good News Translation, like many other contemporary versions, translates verse 17 this way: *'The elders who do good work as leaders should be considered worthy of receiving double pay, especially those who work hard at preaching and teaching.'* In other words, the prosperity of the leaders was clearly a concern for the Apostle Paul who wrote the book. He advocated that certain leaders should receive double pay!

Using further context, we can read again from 1 Timothy and find that in chapter 3 verses 2 and 3 that: *'A bishop then must be blameless, the husband of one wife, vigilant, sober, of good behavior, given to hospitality, apt to teach; 3 Not given to wine, no striker, not greedy of filthy lucre; but patient, not a brawler, not covetous.'* The prosperity doubters might emphasize *'not greedy for filthy lucre,'* to which the 'Word of Faith' movement responds, we agree! The movement, which is practical in its Biblical application, will then continue to point out that in verse 2, it explains that a bishop ought to be *'given to hospitality.'* Well, how can you offer hospitality if you don't have enough to share with others? Prosperity facilitates our ability to offer hospitality. Therefore, a lack of prosperity is clearly an obstacle to hospitality.

Jesus teaches in Luke's Gospel that believers ought to: *'Give, and it shall be given unto you; good measure, pressed down, and shaken together, and running over, shall men give into your bosom. For with the same measure that ye mete withal it shall be measured to you again'* (Luke 6:38). Copeland has taken Biblical verses as a foundation for his life and ministry. Here we can read an example of how he applies the Bible to his life: 'While I was in Ohio, God dealt with me about the television ministry. At that time, I could not understand, or see, with my own mind how it would work financially, but I had learned long before not to back off for his reason. I knew the Lord could work it out. It didn't matter how it operated or what the financial details were, I knew there was only one way to succeed—by giving. Then the thought flashed across my mind, *"No man has given until he has given all he has,"* and the first thing I saw was my twin-engine airplane. Well, cold chills ran up and down my spine! That little plane was my pride and joy. I had tithed and believed God for it, and He had given it to me as a tool of this ministry. Because of this, it really meant a lot to me. Then I realized that I had to get rid of it. I couldn't afford to let it come between God and me, so I went into prayer and the Lord said, "If you will realize what I am leading you into, you will make an agreement with Me so that I can help you financially. Make Me Lord over your finances." That is exactly what I did. I wrote out an agreement about the airplane and used it to lay up a treasure in heaven for the time to come when I would need it. I didn't want to release that airplane, but I knew that God would not take it without His giving more in return. My faith dictated that God's Word was true, so I disciplined my thinking to get in line with my faith (instead of my fear) and I wrote out this agreement: "On the fourth day of October 1971, I give my airplane to the Lord to be sold and the money put into preaching the Word of God on television and in any other manner possible." I made this covenant with the Lord according to Luke 6:38, *"Give, and it shall be given unto you...again,"* and Mark 10:30, *"But he shall receive an hundredfold now in this time."* The agreement also contained this statement: "I freely give this money from the sale of the airplane, and I expect the return on it.' (1974, pp.65,66). The 'Word of Faith' movement have employed this strategy of giving. Critics often have a disdain towards the encouragement to give by ministers but here we can see that Jesus encourages giving and it comes with a promise, this is part of God's economy and financial strategy. The 'Word of Faith' movement has shown great Biblical insight and also integrity in believing and applying these words. Copeland understands that believers are 'Blessed to be a blessing,' Jesus' words are foundational in this emphasis.

The movement believe in the following verse as one of the Biblical promises of their prosperity: *'The blessing of the Lord, it maketh rich, and he addeth no sorrow with it'* (Proverbs 10:22). *'The blessing'* is a key concept within the 'Word of Faith' movement. Let's look at this from within the New Testament and view Galatians 3:13 and 14 which clearly promise *'the blessing'* for New Testament believers: *'Christ hath redeemed us from the curse of the law, being made a curse for us: for it is written, Cursed is every one that hangeth on a tree: 14 That the blessing of Abraham might come on the Gentiles through Jesus Christ; that we might receive the promise of the Spirit through faith.'* In response to these verses Copeland teaches that, 'Jesus bore the curse of the law in our behalf. He beat Satan and took away his power. Consequently, there is no reason for you to live under the curse of the law, no reason for you to live in poverty of any kind. Many born-again believer's live in spiritual poverty, spiritual malnutrition. They are mighty, spiritual supermen in the embryo but not in growing an ounce because they are not being properly fed. Spiritual growth comes only by feeding and acting on the Word of God. *"Desire the sincere milk of the word, that ye may grow thereby"* (1 Peter 2:2).' (1974, p.44).

We can see that *'the blessing'* of Abraham is promised and the promise of the Holy Spirit through faith. The promise of the Holy Spirit can be understood from the New Testament as being filled with the Holy Spirit, being under the Spirit's control and producing the fruit of the Holy Spirit. This is the blessed life. This is not limited to material prosperity but the realm of spiritual prosperity, which impacts everything. In understanding *'the blessing'* of Abraham and the promised material prosperity, we need to go back into the Old Testament and Genesis 12 verses 2 and 3 which detail the promise of God to Abram: *'And I will make of thee a great nation, and I will bless thee, and make thy name great; and thou shalt be a blessing: 3 And I will bless them that bless thee, and curse him that curseth thee: and in thee shall all families of the earth be blessed.'* As Abram who became Abraham was blessed, his blessing has now come on all believers in Jesus.

As previously mentioned, Copeland often describes himself as 'Blessed to be a blessing,' here we can read from where this understanding is rooted: *'Even as Abraham believed God, and it was accounted to him for righteousness. 7 Know ye therefore that they which are of faith, the same are the children of Abraham. 8 And the scripture, foreseeing that God would justify the heathen through faith, preached before the gospel unto Abraham, saying, In thee shall all nations be blessed. 9 So then they which be of faith are blessed with faithful Abraham.'* (Galatians 3:6-9). *'The blessing'* is for the children of faith and the 'Word of Faith' movement have accepted this as theirs.

Definition of Kenneth Copeland's prosperity doctrine

Copeland understands that 'Prosperity' impacts the whole of a person. He has taken care not to limit the understanding of prosperity to financial wealth. Prosperity rather, is for the whole of a person. He explains that,

'True prosperity is the ability to use God's power to meet the needs of mankind in any realm of life' (1974, p.21). He further details that, 'Man is a spirit. He has a soul, consisting of his mind, will, and emotions, and he lives in a body (1985, p.29). Therefore, there exists according to Copeland 'spiritual, mental, and physical prosperity,' which every Christian has a right to experience because of the work of Jesus in establishing the 'New Covenant.'

Spiritual Prosperity:

'Spiritual prosperity' according to Copeland, consists of being reborn as a Christian. He teaches: 'When you accept Jesus as your Savior and make him Lord of your life, your spirit is reborn and brought into fellowship with your Heavenly Father. This puts you in the position to receive from Him all that is promised in His Word' (1985, p.29).

This really is the starting point for total prosperity, without this having taken place, prospering in your physical body and soul realm is not guaranteed. However, once you do prosper in the spiritual realm, you then have access to prosper in the other realms of life.

The prosperity of the Soul: (Mind, Will, and Emotions)

Regarding the soul, Copeland suggests that: 'To prosper in the soul, you must be able to control your mind, will and emotions' (1985, p.29). He approaches the mind, will, and emotions separately and offers a prosperity perspective for each.

Regarding the mind, he suggests: 'Just because you have accumulated a large amount of knowledge does not mean that your mind is prosperous. The prosperity of the mind comes when you use the information that has been acquired when you are controlling your mind instead of your mind controlling you' (1985, p.29-30). This teaching is a testimony to the discipleship open to believers, as the apostle, Paul suggests: *'I beseech you, therefore, brethren, by the mercies of God, that ye present your bodies a living sacrifice, holy, acceptable unto God, which is your reasonable service. 2 And be not conformed to this world: but be ye transformed by the renewing of your mind, that ye may prove what is that good, and acceptable, and perfect, will of God'* (Romans 12:1,2). The sacrificed believer is transformed by a renewed mind to prove the will of God. When this happens, the mind prospers and as we can see, this impacts the whole of the person.

In respect to the will he teaches that: 'When a man's soul is prosperous, his will is in line with God's will' (1985, p.31). Within this, he is highlighting again the need for a Biblical based perspective. For Copeland and the 'Word of Faith' movement, similar to the historical church, God's will is explicitly revealed in 'His Word,' the Bible.

With regard to the prosperity of a person's emotions, Copeland suggests that: 'To remain prosperous in the soul, we should not be motivated or controlled by our feelings' (1985, p.32). Copeland goes on to suggest that: 'A prosperous soul must keep its emotions in line with the Word of God' (1985, p.32).

Physical Prosperity:

Regarding 'physical prosperity' Copeland teaches that: 'When you are walking in the Word of God, you will prosper and be in health. It is His will for us to be made whole spirit, soul and body' (1985, p.34). Copeland believes prosperity is the will of God for all Christians (Copeland 1974, p.43). His conclusions are Biblical, one key scripture is from his exegesis of Luke 4:16-21 and especially the emphasis Jesus gave to the preaching of the Gospel to the poor in verse 18, *'The Spirit of the Lord is upon me, because he hath anointed me to preach the gospel to the poor'* (Luke 4:18) (Copeland 1985, p.11). The Gospel to the poor involves the potential for a change in their circumstances, so that they would not be poor any longer. Indeed, they can be blessed and rich instead of cursed and poor, good news for oppressed people who live in poor and marginalized conditions.

There are many Christian teachings that regard material wealth with some amount of caution. Copeland explains that this type of perspective is what poverty-stricken people have been continually taught (1985, p.11) and therefore, it is these poor people, the very ones to whom Jesus promised 'Good news,' who have been robbed of the full Gospel message.

Foundation principals of Kenneth Copeland's prosperity doctrine

Copeland's theological position holds to a universality for those who believe, this is seen within his 'Laws of Prosperity' (Hunt 1998, p.275). For example, in 1986 when preaching to 4,000 evangelists from 41 African countries he pointed out that prosperity isn't American, it is universally available to all those who will follow the correct biblical principles

(1974, p.32). Copeland cited the example of a church in poverty-ridden Mozambique. At a time when food supplies and other essential items were scarce, this church was practicing the 'Laws of Prosperity.' Such was the subsequent success, that the Mozambique government commented that their gospel message was the only thing giving the people any hope (1985, p.28). This is a remarkable and tangible example of the impact of embracing a Biblical prosperity doctrine. Dry western theology had nothing to directly help the poor and needy people of Mozambique. For Copeland, his belief and its authenticity are proven by tangible results. His far-reaching ministry has impacted the poorest of people in real ways, firstly with a transformed mindset. This has helped many believe for better and subsequently receive from that belief. It's also worth noting that Copeland has provided significant practical support with food, education, medical provisions and much more.

The critics of the 'Word of Faith' movement, on the other hand, do not seem to have the same level of practical ministry experience and impact. Hanegraaff, McConnell and Peters for example, have established their reputations not by establishing churches or preaching the Gospel, but rather by pushing a mythology of criticisms. As we have seen they have been rightly accused of characterization and of holding polarized views.

Once God can be recognized as a loving Father, it becomes easier to accept that the prosperity of His children is an important factor in creating a 'Covenant' with them. Whether it was the 'Old' or the 'New Covenant,' both clearly have provision for prosperity in them. An essential factor in Copeland's prosperity teachings and one central to his 'Laws of Prosperity,' is known as 'seed-faith'. His early mentor Oral Roberts is regarded as originally emphasizing this (1974, p.42). Copeland has expounded his 'seed-faith' teaching from biblical verses such as Luke 6:38, *'Give and it shall be given unto you'* and Mark 10:30, *'but he shall receive an hundredfold now in this time.'* These principals according to Copeland, if employed today, mean that Christians can exercise faith, sow a seed and thereafter be confident that God will grow it (1974, p.42). As Coleman has observed, for Copeland prosperity is a responsibility, not merely a potential benefit of faith. Coleman quotes the following: 'you wouldn't think well of a farmer who planted seeds, then let his crop rot in the field while people are starving. It's just as irresponsible to give financial seeds and not to receive a harvest from them, while there are people starving to hear the gospel' (Coleman 2000, p.188). Bishop Newbigin has suggested that 'the church today cannot without guilt absolve itself from the responsibility, where it sees the possibility, of seeking to shape the public life of nations and the global ordering of industry and commerce in the light of the Christian faith'

(Newbigin 1986, p.129). It ought to be pointed out that this is precisely what Copeland's prosperity doctrine seeks to do. Through missions, and the provision of practical aid, Copeland has used his blessing to bless others. Also, the teaching causes local people who are 'Word of Faith' believers, to be leaders, business owners, entrepreneurs and to believe for success through faith in God's promises. Of the worldwide ministries that exist, Copeland has come extremely close to meeting the expectations of the above Bishop Newbigin quotation. Therefore, within a capitalistic society such as America, a Biblical prosperity message is able to employ the Correlation Method cited by Ballard and Pritchard (1996, p.121).

Within the Correlation Method, theology is offered as 'a way of speaking to modern debates by identifying contemporary human needs and preoccupations and then finding the theology which could interact with the language used in those debates' (1996, p.121). Copeland and the 'Word of Faith' movement, unlike the many denominational churches, have helped to educate and engage people in a practical way towards prosperity and health. At the most basic level, every right-thinking human being desires a certain level of prosperity and health for themselves and their loved ones. These Biblical truths have helped communicate that which is relevant today, for large numbers of people globally.

Many commentators on Copeland and the 'Word of Faith' movement, such as Taylor and others suggest that, 'Some see the 'Prosperity Gospel' as serving the interests of that style of extreme capitalism being promoted by the USA around the world' (Taylor 2003, p.29). However, they seem to have confused Copeland with the secular capitalistic philosophy of prosperity, and this is simply inaccurate. The 'Prosperity Gospel' Copeland preaches for example, involves adopting a significantly generous attitude to giving, something that modern secular capitalism isn't known for. Copeland writes: 'See yourself giving to the needs that are around you. Remember, meeting the needs of others with God's power is what prosperity is all about' (Copeland 1985, p.61). This is diametrically opposite from what is often understood within capitalistic prosperity, this is Biblical prosperity, employing an entirely different foundation.

Furthermore, Copeland sees the world's financial system as 'Babylonian,' in that it is predicated on a 'fiat' money system of debt. 'Fiat' money is derived from the Latin 'fiat' meaning 'let it be done.' It is used in the sense of a decree regarding currency existing without intrinsic value or any commodities backing it. It began to dominate world economics in the 20th century and in America for example, it gained momentum when the gold standard ended under President Richard Nixon in 1971.

Influences on Copeland

The result of covenant blessing in Old Testament theology, is repeatedly victory over enemies and material prosperity: *'That I may cause those that love me to inherit substance; and I will fill their treasures'* (Proverbs 8:21). The blessing of Abraham continued through Isaac and Jacob, and the seed multiplied through their descendants. Abraham was neither Arab nor Jew, it was his grandson, Jacob, whom God renamed Israel (Genesis 32:28) and it was Jacob's sons who then became the twelve tribes of Israel. One of those tribes was Judah and is from where the name 'Jew' is derived. The promise to Abraham was that the world would be blessed by Abraham's seed, this fulfillment was found through Jesus Christ.

For the 'Word of Faith' movement, financial prosperity is rightly founded from the Abrahamic covenant. The believer enters this blessing through the atonement. Hagin confirms the New Testament's promise when he writes, 'Abraham's blessing is ours! ... Abraham's blessing was a threefold blessing. The first thing God promised Abraham was that He was going to make him rich. "Do you mean God is going to make us all rich?" Yes, that's what I mean. "Do you mean He's going to make us all millionaires?" No, I didn't say that. But He is going to make us rich. You may not understand what the word "rich" means. The dictionary says it means "a full supply" or "abundantly provided for." Praise God, there is a full supply in Christ!' (1983, p.5)

It has been observed that Hagin's teaching and influence have had a great impact into South Africa through the Rhema churches. They have been considered, 'the most compassionate and generous Christians' (Pousson 1992, p.144) in South Africa. A local Pastor testifies that 'Far from abandoning their responsibilities towards the poor, these Christians see it as their God-given duty to do what they can to alleviate poverty and not just through the proclamation of 'prosperity,' but in practical giving!' (1992, p.144).

Copeland started his ministerial training as a student at Oral Robert's University in 1967. Roberts contributed towards the 'Word of Faith' understanding of prosperity and writes: 'Prosperity is the possession of everything you need for yourself and loved ones with enough surplus to give to those who need help. If you have only the bare necessities, you are not prosperous. And if you have all the sufficiencies of life but no more, that is not prosperity. But, if you have everything you need with something left over for the poor, that is prosperity. If, after you have paid the tithe, you have enough for offerings to spread the gospel and help the needy, that is prosperity' (1963, p.51).

Copeland and the 'Word of Faith' movement have the Bible as their foundation, this is their final authority. Whilst Copeland has been influenced by Hagin, Roberts, Kenyon, and others, his final authority has clearly been the Bible. We can see for example, how he responds to people who claim they can't help feeling fearful anxious thoughts; He says, '... I don't believe that because the Bible says: *'Be anxious for nothing, but in everything by prayer and supplication, with thanksgiving, let your requests be made known to God; 7 and the peace of God, which surpasses all understanding, will guard your hearts and minds through Christ Jesus'* (Philippians 4:6,7) (2011, p.284). In other words, when the Bible says that a person can prosper mentally by not being fearful or anxious, Copeland believes the Biblical promise. The person has simply failed to yield to the Biblical promise.

Copeland and the 'Word of Faith' movement confirm that the blessing of God is for all believers, this is foundational. The title of Copelands 2011 book on the blessing, is taken straight from the scripture: *'The blessing of the LORD, it maketh rich, and he addeth no sorrow with it'* (Proverbs 10:22).

Copeland's prosperity emphasis

According to Copeland the 'words' or 'contract' Christians now have known as the 'New Testament,' ought to be experienced through faith, by every Christian. One of Copeland's greatest strengths, therefore, is his reliance on the Bible and its relevance to 21st century Christianity. When the 'New Testament' promises for example: *'Beloved, I wish above all things that mayest prosper and be in health, even as thy soul prospereth'* (3 John 2), Copeland takes this as a direct mandate from God to be healthy and to prosper. As does Hagin, who suggests regarding this verse, 'I believe his intent and meaning was to refer to three distinct areas of life, material, physical, and spiritual. His fervent desire was that we should thrive and flourish, or prosper, in every aspect of our being' (2000, p13).

In Copeland's missiological view, he believes that the poor have been patronized historically, he is not alone in this perspective and academics such as Bosch agree with this view (Bosch 1991, p.308). Whilst missionaries might live well fed and in relative comfort, the message they've proclaimed is often one that is content with lack and poverty. For Copeland, missionaries who have promoted lack and poverty have misrepresented the true Gospel.

Copeland's foundational point is that the church has not continued in Jesus' commission to preach the gospel to the poor. He concludes that until it does preach the 'good news' to the poor the church isn't preaching the full Gospel message at all (Copeland 1985, p.11). He suggests that the Gospel to the poor 'is that Jesus has come and (therefore) they don't have to be poor anymore' (1985, p.11). This rationale from Copeland asks the question, what else could Jesus have meant in declaring 'good news' to poor, other than now because of Him, there can be a change in their material circumstances. Now, they can be freed from the evil ravages of poverty. Any other reading of the text might well be betraying the modern western bias of self-reliance, which is taken from a position of material abundance.

In other words, it is only first world rich countries who seem to object to Biblical prosperity. The poor are often very pleased to hear and accept this message of salvation and material hope.

Supernatural prosperity

Copeland understands that within the supernatural atonement of Christ, sickness, poverty, and the curse was replaced with healing, wealth, and the blessing of God. He bases his argument on texts such as: *'...though he was rich, yet for your sakes, he became poor, that ye through his poverty might be rich'* (2 Corinthians 8:9). The Transliteration of the Greek, *'might be rich'* is the word plouteó. As Copeland has observed, it means to become rich, to abound and to have many resources. Copeland's Biblical exegesis comes from a desire to see those he ministers to prosper. However, first of all, this was a revelation he needed to understand for himself. He explains how the following verses impacted his life as a student minister in 1966 when they, 'sent shock waves through my spirit' (2011, p.20): *'Christ hath redeemed us from the curse of the law, being made a curse for us: for it is written, Cursed is every one that hangeth on a tree: 14 That the blessing of Abraham might come on the Gentiles through Jesus Christ; that we might receive the promise of the Spirit through faith. 29 And if ye be Christ's, then are ye Abraham's seed, and heirs according to the promise'* (Galatians 3:13,14,29) (2011, p.20). Copeland has observed that his strong emphasis on the blood covenant of the New Covenant, was helped because of his American Indian heritage and their awareness of the strength of blood covenants (2011, p.21).

Copeland began to study the Bible and it became clear that Abraham was a rich man. Therefore, he concluded by the study of Galatians 3:14, that the blessing of Abraham was his, because of Jesus' blood sacrifice. Therefore, he started to believe along Biblical lines such as: *'The blessing of the Lord, it maketh rich, and he addeth no sorrow with it'* (Proverbs 10:22). Bosch, the noted missiological academic, agrees with Copeland's general critique regarding traditional missionary work, for example, Bosh claimed that the enlightenment missionaries often patronized and pitied their listeners and took the role of 'the guardians of the less-developed races' (Bosch 1991, p.308). However, despite Bosch's critique of the Enlightenment period, his conclusions regarding prosperity would probably be very different to Copeland's. Nussbaum for example, has observed Bosch's caution regarding supernatural events such as healing (Nussbaum 2005, p.151). However, for Copeland, supernatural events are foundational to his theology. There is a worldwide continuity of people from all branches of the Church who recognize that Christian ministry is to preach, teach, and heal. It is in doing this, that we follow in the footsteps of our Lord Jesus Christ: *'And Jesus went about all Galilee, teaching in their synagogues, and preaching the gospel of the kingdom, and healing all manner of sickness and all manner of disease among the people'* (Matthew 4:23). Therefore, if we don't do this we are simply not following in Jesus' footsteps and the mandate He gave us, is being ignored.

The traditional denominations tendency towards liberal theology has promoted a spiritual detachment that often accompanies their academia. It offers an impotent position to those in need of Biblical supernatural help. For example, in the area of physical healing, liberalism often only concedes hope towards an 'inner healing.' This popular position can ultimately, only be understood as a popular form of 'respectable' Biblical rebellion, or even theological cowardice. What else would purport to follow Jesus and not even consider supernatural healing as an option? Academia, since the Enlightenment, through the religion that it shapes, produces intellectuals, who know about God but often fail to truly know God and live in His power. Surely, 2 Timothy 3:5 offers a clear warning on this matter, *'Having a form of godliness, but denying the power thereof: from such turn away.'*

In contrast to this, the 'Word of Faith' movement has sought to promote adherence to Biblical standards as a mandate for life. In certain positive ways, it could be understood that Copeland's theology is similar to a Third-World theology. Clearly Copeland's theology was not born directly out of a Third-World context, after all, Copeland's context was Texas. However, in Copeland's formative years, much of West Texas was a poverty-ridden, poorly educated, dirt-farming environment and as such, it had similarities to aspects of the Third World. It is interesting to consider the observation by

Bosch that 'First-World Christians should study Third-World Theologies' (Bosch 1991, p.428). Bosch recognizes the lack of real-life practicalities within formal theological western colleges. They often seem to forget that Jesus was a provider of what the people needed in everyday life, wisdom, water, food and healing for example.

Copeland and the 'Word of Faith' movement's prosperity teaching rely on a supernatural perspective which is often at odds with much in the modern, rational, mainstream theological perspectives. It has been noted by anthropologist Kraft for example that, 'when a worldview is supernaturalistic, it is common for people to regard material goods as signs of the blessing of God' (Kraft1996, p.189).

Purpose of prosperity according to Kenneth Copeland

Copeland has suggested that 'the whole purpose for gainful employment and prosperity is to take God's laws, prosper by them and then do something about the poverty in the rest of the world' (1985, p.16). For Copeland, this is an explicit expression of the 'Kingdom of God' through the church and He suggests that: 'God wants you to prosper, not just to put food on your table, but also to reach out and help provide food for someone else' (1985, p.46). Copeland also teaches, 'true prosperity is the ability to meet the needs of mankind in any realm of life, wealth and power cannot answer every need' (1985, p.33). When Copeland refers to 'any realm of life' he's pointing towards the earlier mentioned three areas of human life and the ability, as he describes it, for the prosperity of spirit, soul, and body (1985, p.46). In these definitions, Copeland shows that his understanding of prosperity is to have resources, not for selfish gain, but rather to meet the needs of others. Copeland's views are focused, Biblical, and demonstrably beneficial for many people.

Theological theories can be interesting, but theology ultimately must find its expression in the reality of the mission of the church. Copeland, and the 'Word of Faith' movement have had a significant impact into a vast number of people globally. They have funded great relief for the poorest of peoples and this would not have been possible without their own prosperity. From a standing start, the 'Word of Faith' networks have grown into a significant worldwide arm of the Christian church. It might well be said of Copeland, that his teachings would pass Bishop Tom Wright's acid test for all theology. Wright suggests, through Aquinas' summary: 'Theology is taught by God, teaches of God, and leads to God' (Wright 1993, p.681).

Copeland has criticized greed and the western desire to use prosperity as a means of selfish comfort especially the 'provision of more conveniences and luxuries' (1985, p.46). However, within the same page of his 1985 book 'Prosperity: The Choice is Yours,' he admits that he had been 'guilty' at one time of pursuing the comforts of wealth, but subsequently, he has not only changed but 'repented' of these actions (1985, p.46). This is a striking admission which shows a humility, honesty, and the authentic vulnerability of a minister of the Gospel of Jesus Christ. He is aware of the potential harm within material possessions but rather than running away from these dangers, he has concentrated on diffusing them through a Biblical approach. Therefore, perhaps this is why we can see so much of an emphasis on giving within his teachings. Rather than a well which can only offer limited supplies to people, Copeland insists we are to be more like pipes lines, that have a seemingly unlimited supply of resources (1974, p.61).

Copeland has observed that within missionary thinking there has been a tradition which has universally supported a meager existence and even equates such, as a manifestation of sanctification and piety (1985, p.14). In another similar observation, he comments regarding poverty that: '... it's in religion, not in the Bible. It was put into Christianity as a religion during the Dark Ages when the Word was taken from the people and put away in monasteries. Poverty oaths were fed into Christianity when the religious hierarchy took over; the men operating it were not born-again men' (1996, p.26). Whilst poverty oaths were within the doctrines of many groups including, the Franciscans (who cited Augustine) and Bonaventure. However, it should be noted that these doctrines, even at the time of surfacing, were not without significant objectors as Lambert has pointed out (Lambert 1961, p.143).

People such as Gort have, like Copeland, observed the ongoing issues of poverty and he has pointed towards two-thirds of the world that live within what he classifies as the 'structural evil' of poverty (Gort 1995, p.203). He points the finger of blame towards geopolitical and economic structures. However, as we have noted in the earlier mentioned Mozambique example from Copeland, a Biblical theology is able to overcome the evils in the world, if it is employed correctly. Then, as we have cited, even governments can take notice. Surely, this is the Kingdom manifesting on planet Earth in accordance with God's will. This brings the integrity of our manifestation to the prayer Jesus taught: *'Thy kingdom come; Thy will be done in earth, as it is in heaven'* (Matthew 6:10).

Chapter 4

The 'Word of Faith' movement

What is the 'Word of Faith' movement?

The 'Word of Faith' movement derives its name from the Biblical passage of Romans chapter 10 verse 8 which reads, *'...the word of faith that we preach.'* It is established out of an informal network of Christian churches and teaching ministries, with roots in Pentecostal or Charismatic traditions. It is recognizably within historic Christian beliefs; exponents preach a message of salvation through Jesus Christ as a central theme. The Bible is regarded as authoritative, and a life of discipline is promoted with traditional Christian views on ethics and morality. The movement emphasizes subjects such as the power of words, believers' authority, healing, prosperity, Kingdom, and most importantly walking in Biblical love.

Today the 'Word of Faith' movement is one of the most influential branches of modern Christianity worldwide. The observation that it has been the subject of ongoing attacks does not necessarily mean anything substantial. Most new and significant movements within church history have caused a stir, the early Pentecostals, the Methodists, the Reformers, the list goes all the way back to Biblical times and the early church itself, which was regarded as a Jewish sect (Burkett 2002: p. 3). Today, for example, John Wesley is one of the most revered of historical Christian figures, yet in his life, he was highly criticized, physically attacked, and regularly threatened with violence. The following observation about Wesley has been made, it could equally be applied to the 'Word of Faith' movement and leaders such as Copeland: 'They were denounced as promulgators of strange doctrines, fomenters of religious disturbances;

as blind fanatics, leading people astray, claiming miraculous gifts' [Lane, 2018].

The movement teaches that through the atonement of Christ Jesus, provision was made for mankind to live within the family of God, in prosperity of spirit, soul, (which is defined as being the mind, will, and emotions) and the physical body (Copeland 1985, p.29). An emphasis on prosperity is nothing new in the church, it can clearly be shown to be entirely Biblical and historical. For example, John Calvin suggested that poverty was to be equated with a lack of favor with God. In time, this view progressed to associate prosperity as a sign that a person was truly saved (Swatos 1998, p. 373). Calvin's view was so strong that it goes far beyond most modern exponents of prosperity today. Following on from Calvin, we can find another key tenant of the 'Word of Faith' within the work of the 19th century revivalist Charles Finney, we see that he, similarly to Copeland, was committed to employing 'all means' to promote the Gospel (Swatos 1998:513). The 'Word of Faith' movement's desire to use 'all means,' has been helped by their acceptance of prosperity. For the 'Word of Faith' movement, 'all means' often includes the use of vehicles such as satellite television, radio, book and magazine publications, and the use of time-saving airplanes for the efficiency and freedom of transportation.

The 'Word of Faith' movement has become one of the most influential branches of modern Christianity. Critics have accused the movement of distorting Scripture and promoting a manipulative brand of 'American Televangelism' around the world. Many of the most combative arguments have come from those within mainstream denominations and the movement has often been referred to in derogatory terms such as, 'The Gospel of greed,' or the 'Name it and Claim it Gospel' (Perriman 2003, p. xviii). It has repeatedly been suggested by critics that the 'Word of Faith' movement ought to be viewed as a cultic blend of metaphysics and Christianity. As we have previously noted, these arguments have been presented by Daniel McConnell, Hank Hanegraaff, Peters and other subsequent critics who have largely followed McConnell's original mythology. The premises of these attacks are flawed in both methodology and accuracy. People such as William DeArteaga, Joe McIntyre, and the important Perriman Report, have suggested that the movement's roots are to be found within evangelical, charismatic Christian denominations.

It has been suggested that 'Word of Faith' exponents often appear to have all the trappings of a highly successful life, including financial wealth and power. In response to this, the Perriman Report has observed that those representing the mainstream church have historically viewed the 'Word of

Faith' movement with 'ingrained and largely unexamined moral revulsion' (2003, p.231). In using the word 'unexamined,' the Perriman Report is highlighting the historical tendency that exists against the movement, towards prejudice and what it calls a 'spiritual snobbery' (2003, p.231). The critics betray their prejudice because while the trappings of prosperity might be unusual to many traditional western Christian ministries, anthropologist Charles Kraft is among many who have noted that 'when a worldview is supernaturalistic, it is common for people to regard material goods as signs of the blessing of God' (1996, p.189). The Perriman Report comments that traditional African religion is meant to ensure fertility, abundance, and longevity, and so wealth and success are natural signs of supernatural blessings (2003, p.7). These perspectives can be well observed within the previously mentioned ministry of reformer John Calvin and the 'Word of Faith' movement alike.

Furthermore, it has been suggested by Gifford that the speed at which African churches were able to go through processes of indigenization with the 'Word of Faith' movement, has been due in part to the African Church's lack of Western asceticism (Perriman 2003, p.7). These observations are helpful in highlighting positions that are evident and validated in both the bible texts themselves and church history.

The expectation throughout 'Word of Faith' ministries is very similar, as the Perriman Report has observed, 'God will bless the church' (2003, p.12). This was also clearly the mindset of Biblical peoples, and as anthropologists such as Kraft have noted (1996, p.189), is still often found around the world, mostly outside of western secular societies.

As mentioned earlier John Calvin, who was often known as 'Defender of Christianity,' was likewise a definite believer in prosperity (Swatos 1998, p.373). The benefits, blessing, and expectations towards a God given financial prosperity, seem to have been lost to the critics of the 'Word of Faith' movement. In the main, they have also been lost to much of the western church. To some degree this might be because western churches are still influenced by ascetic traditions and their connection between vows of poverty and spirituality. These traditions are juxtaposed with a comparatively prosperous 'goods' orientated western culture. From a shallow perspective, the shunning of a 'goods' orientated culture, might appear to be a move of spiritual intent.

McConnell suggests that within the 'Word of Faith' movement the doctrine of prosperity is a 'carnal accommodation to the crass materialism of American culture' (1988, p.179). However, considering the above-mentioned observations from different cultures, anthropology, and the

Bible itself, McConnell's conclusion appears overly simplistic. It lacks an appreciation of a more comprehensive historical Christian worldview and seems bereft of any recognition of the potential legitimacy of Biblical prosperity.

The movement is influential because many of its exponents have worldwide satellite television broadcasts that daily reach into billions of homes. The estimated potential reach of the Trinity Broadcasting Network alone, is over 2 billion. The ministries have annual turnovers running into many millions of dollars, and they often have a publishing arm that produces an array of media products including DVD's, magazines, and books. There are significant organizational skills employed in running these ministries. The main historical hubs for the movement are the ICFM founded in 1979 and Hagin's own association the RMAI established in 1985. On the ICFM website, there is a section entitled, 'Our Beliefs.' These beliefs are consistent with expected Christian views, under the heading of *'The One True God'* for example, they write: 'We believe there is one God, Creator of all things, Who is infinitely perfect and eternally existent in three persons, God the Father, God the Son, and God the Holy Spirit.' They share this view with many other Christian groups including the Evangelical Free Church of America [EFCA, 2018]. Their other shared beliefs are well used and commonly held within many churches. Let's look at a sample of a further three:

Under *'The Holy Scriptures'* they write: We believe the Scriptures, both Old and New Testament, are the inspired Word of God and are the revelation of God to man, the infallible Divine and final authority for all Christian faith and life.

Under *'The Ministry of the Holy Spirit'* they write: We believe the ministry of the Holy Spirit is to glorify the Lord Jesus Christ. During this age He has been sent to indwell, guide, instruct and empower the believer for godly living and service. The Holy Spirit bestows the spiritual gifts of: (1) Word of Wisdom, (2) Word of Knowledge, (3) Faith, (4) Gifts of Healings, (5) Working of Miracles, (6) Prophecy, (7) Discerning of Spirits, (8) Diverse Kinds of Tongues, (9) Interpretation of Tongues in and among believers on the earth since the Day of Pentecost and continuing until our Lord's return.

Under *'The Baptism in the Holy Spirit'* they write: We believe the Baptism in the Holy Spirit is granted to all believers who ask for this experience. We believe this experience is distinct from and follows the new birth. Every believer can and should be filled with the Holy Spirit and speak in tongues. We believe the Baptism in the Holy Spirit is witnessed by the initial physical sign of speaking with other tongues as the Spirit of God gives utterance.

This small selection of beliefs from the ICFM website shows that they are entirely consistent with believers from an array of church backgrounds.

In expounding on what salvation consists of, the movement's critics suggest that it has deviated from traditional Christian teachings and into an emphasis on prosperity, positive confession, and supernatural healing. These subjects are Biblical and are also part of the 'Word of Faith' movement, but the critics deliberately leave out significant portions of the 'Word of Faith' movement's teaching. For example, the movement's founder, Kenneth Hagin has repeatedly taught that while faith is important, to love is even more so. In his book 'Love The Way To Victory' he concludes that 'If people criticize me, I'm not going to get all flustered and upset about it and miss God's blessings in my life. I'm going to stay in an attitude of love and do what the Bible says' (2005, p.227).

The critics haven't attempted to estimate what percentage of teaching within the movement is given to different subjects. This would be a difficult task, but it would be helpful in that it would demonstrate the broader theological emphasis of the movement and confirm their strongest emphasis, which is Biblical love. Kenneth and Gloria Copeland for example, have repeatedly followed Hagin in teaching that the Christian life is the 'Love walk' (2011, p.293). This teaching was based on a verse of scripture and has been used by Kenneth and Gloria Copeland as a summary of a significant portion of their ministry, it reads: *'Owe no man anything, but to love one another: for he that loveth another hath fulfilled the law'* (Romans 13:8). This verse was the impetus behind their focus on promoting living debt free and walking in love.

Critics of the 'Word of Faith' movement claim that the movement's theological emphasis is not in line with historic Christian teachings. However, it would be more accurate to assert that the 'Word of Faith' movement's emphasis, might not be in line with the critics' church traditions especially cessationism. This point will be further demonstrated within our assessment of the atonement and the critics' false claims.

The 'Word of Faith' movement believes that Jesus Christ made provision for mankind to live a victorious life through the atonement. Believers can live devoid of sickness and poverty. The movement cites many Biblical examples regarding prosperity and the other benefits of being in a relationship with God. Two of these key verses are found within the book of Galatians: *'Christ hath redeemed us from the curse of the law, being made a curse for us: for it is written, Cursed is every one that hangeth on a tree: 14 That the blessing of Abraham might come on the Gentiles through Jesus Christ; that we might receive the promise of the Spirit through faith'* (Galatians 3:13,14). Regarding these verses, Copeland explains: 'The day I actually grasped what those verses were saying, it hit me like a freight train coming through a tunnel: I am the seed of Abraham! I am the product of a blood-sworn oath, a covenant cut between God and His firstborn Son. The LORD Jesus Christ is my blood brother! Because of my American Indian background, I knew something about blood covenants' (2011, p.21).

The blessing of Abraham mentioned above is given for believers. To understand what this means further, we can consider Genesis 12 verses 2 and 3: *'And I will make of thee a great nation, and I will bless thee, and make thy name great; and thou shalt be a blessing: 3 And I will bless them that bless thee, and curse him that curseth thee: and in thee shall all families of the earth be blessed.'* 'Word of Faith' teachers such as Kenneth and Gloria Copeland, have somewhat coined the phrase, 'Blessed to be a blessing.' This is based on the promise given to Abraham and passed on to Christian believers as shown in Galatians 3. Blessed in every area of life, without limits and without lack, that's what the "Word of Faith' movement has stood for, and indeed, it is what many within the movement have received.

The 'Word of Faith' movement has been the most influential and far-reaching Christian movement since the eighteenth century and the impact of John and Charles Wesley, George Whitfield, and the Methodism movement. Hagin read biographies on these eighteenth-century leaders, and they were a source of inspiration to him (Hagin, 1976). 'Word of Faith' ministries are among the most listened too and published worldwide. Through various outlets, including satellite television, radio, and large publishing houses. Unlike many 'mainstream' denominations which are diminishing in their relevance and numbers, the 'Word of Faith' movement continues to flourish and expand. The movement has encouraged believers to have a foundation on the Bible and faith in Jesus Christ

A brief history of the 'Word of Faith' movement

We will start this history with the movement's founder Kenneth Hagin. Hagin's associates were clearly mainly within the Charismatic and Pentecostal groups, these included healing evangelists such as T. L Osborn, William Branham, and Oral Roberts. In 1963 the Kenneth E. Hagin Evangelistic Association was formed which involved various media outreaches including, Faith Library Publications, which to date has printed in excess of 65 million books and has a monthly magazine for 250,000 subscribers. It is a characteristic of 'Word of Faith' exponents to use radio and satellite television broadcasts to promote the Gospel. Hagin's first radio program for example, which began in 1967, was entitled 'Faith Seminar of the Air' and echoes Kenyon's 1930's program title 'Kenyon's Church of the Air'. Also, through his Rhema Bible College in Oklahoma established in 1974, Hagin has promoted the 'Word of Faith' message through over 40,000 alumni, a high proportion of whom are in full-time Christian ministry. It was during Hagin's ministry that the 'Word of Faith' beliefs took shape as a clear and visible movement. Furthermore, it was also during Hagin's ministry that the movement's teachings became more distinctive and recognizable, in part, this was because of Hagin's large-scale publishing of material. He was further aided by great improvements within mass media communications. By the early 1980's Hagin's ministry was flourishing but soon critics such as McConnell and Dave Hunt arose and the 'Word of Faith' teaching, was being characterized by the critical mythology makers, in terms such as the: 'Greed Gospel,' 'Prosperity Gospel,' and the 'Health and Wealth' movement.

The influence of Hagin has been further extended by Kenneth Copeland who has been a devout student of Hagin (1993, p.33). Copeland, who started off preaching in the late 1960's while a student at Oral Robert's University in Tulsa, U.S.A. would often memorize portions from the teachings of Hagin (1993, p.33). In 1979 Copeland's itinerant evangelism and teaching ministry expanded into satellite television and aired 'The Believers Voice of Victory.' This program has rapidly extended its influence and is now broadcast around the world on various satellite networks. It has helped promote Copeland into being the most widely influential of all the 'Word of Faith' exponents. Copeland's 'Word of Faith' colleagues, in turn, have also employed various media avenues and seen significant growth. Some, such as Creflo Dollar, Jesse Duplantis, Jerry Saville, and Bill Winston for example, also have particularly significant worldwide Christian media networks.

The movement has spread throughout the world via informal networks of churches, international conferences, book and magazine publishing, and satellite media broadcasts. In 1979 a significant event happened when leaders of the 'Word of Faith' movement founded the 'International Convention of Faith Ministries (ICFM).' It stated aim is to: 'Hold forth, contend for and propagate the Word of Faith worldwide.' The ICFM along with Hagin's own RMAI have been the main link organizations for many within the 'Word of Faith' movement worldwide.

Hagin's fresh perspective on faith is clear from the title of one of his most famous books, which suggests that when faith is employed, 'You Can Have What You Say' (Perriman 2003, p.3). His ministry has been succeeded by his son Kenneth Hagin Jr., but as the Perriman Report has noted, the true successor to Hagin has been his former student Kenneth Copeland (Perriman 2003, p.4).

There is, and have been, a large collection of similarly well noted ministries connected to the 'Word of Faith' movement including: Charles Capps, Creflo and Taffi Dollar, Jesse and Cathy Duplantis, Norvel Hayes, Joyce Meyer, Keith Moore, John Osteen, Joel and Victoria Osteen, Bishop David Oyedepo, Rick Renner, Jerry Saville, Leroy Thompson, Robert Tilton, and Bill Winston, to name just a few.

The movement got a tremendous boost in 1973 when Paul Crouch founded the Trinity Broadcasting Network (TBN), headquartered in Santa Ana, California. TBN is the world's largest Christian television network and airs on over 5,000 TV stations, 33 international satellites, cable television and the internet. It broadcasts the 'Word of Faith' message globally and with a specifically large capacity into the United States, Europe, Russia, the Middle East, Africa, Australia, New Zealand, the South Pacific, India, Indonesia, Southeast Asia, and South America.

The 'Word of Faith' movement's Pentecostal roots

When we consider what does it mean to be a follower of Jesus? The answer to that question can be found by firstly considering how we would describe someone who was not following Jesus. Therefore, some antonyms for the word follow are disregard, misunderstand and neglect. To honestly follow Jesus therefore, we must have regard, understanding, and pay attention too, His teachings toward us. It is from this level of sincerity and observance, that the 'Word of Faith' movements' roots can be found and understood. The movement's supernatural emphasis is therefore, a commitment to yield to the teaching and commission of Jesus Christ to: go into all the world to preach the gospel, baptize, drive out demons, speak in new tongues and heal the sick (Mark 16:15-18).

Hagin is the Father of the 'Word of Faith' movement, not Kenyon. We have taken a brief overview and history of the 'Word of Faith' movement and Hagin's ministry, to establish this clearly. However, as we have seen it is claimed by critics such as McConnell and Hanegraaff that the roots of the 'Word of Faith' movement have a metaphysical influence through Kenyon.

Therefore, the critics claim in their mythology that the whole movement ought to be classified as 'cultic' and discredited (1995, pp.24-26). However, we are showing categorically within this work that the movement did not have cultic roots. Such conclusions are not merely wrong but given the plethora of evidence, they can only be understood as disingenuous and divisive. For example, one of the attempted links by the critics to the metaphysical cults has been in the emphasis on positive confession and healing. However, it has been shown that the beginnings of positive confession concerning healing can be traced to the work of A. B. Simpson (1843-1919).

Simpson was a well-respected preacher, author, and theologian. He founded the Christian and Missionary Alliance (C&MA), an evangelical denomination with an emphasis on global evangelism. His position is the same as the 'Word of Faith' movement, he wrote, 'We believe that God is healing before any evidence is given. It is to be believed as a present reality and then ventured on. We are to act as if it were already true.' (Barron, p.62) Simpson was a well-educated highly respected minister and he advocated faith contrary to sensory evidence. In this, he was demonstrating that a belief in the Bible's supernatural teaching offered a higher authority than a senses-based rationale. The supernatural emphasis is what the critics seem to challenge the most, and in this, they often betray their own moribund, anti-supernatural, cessationist position.

Hagan would have been influenced by Simpson who was a well noted historical figure by the time Hagin began his ministry. Whilst Kenyon did influence Hagin and other Word of Faith ministers, Hagin is the movement's true 'Father.' This is most obviously seen in the way that Hagin was affectionately known by the 'Word of Faith' movement as, 'Daddy Hagin.'

As we have repeatedly noted, Hanegraaff and McConnell have attempted to align the 'Word of Faith' movement with the metaphysical cults. Hanegraaff, like most of the critics, has followed McConnell and agreed that Kenyon is the movement's 'Father' (1993, p.331) and even more favorable commentators such as DeArteaga, have been persuaded by this (1993, p.200; 1997, p.46). However, the evidence shows clearly that McConnell has created a mythology to discredit the movement and Kenyon as 'Father' is a key component of the mythology. It is important therefore to note that the most scholastic observation of the 'Word of Faith' movement, the Perriman Report, has dated the origins of the 'Word of Faith' movement as being after the Second World War (2003, p. xviii). The report considers the movement to have originated in post-war Pentecostal revivalism (2003, p.77). Bowman, who according to the Perriman Report offers the most academic appraisal, has also concluded that Hagin is the Father of the movement (2001, p.36). Similarly, to the Perriman Report, Bowman also dates the movement's origins after the Second World War and shows that the movements roots are to be found, not in metaphysical cults but in Pentecostalism (2001, p.11; 2003, p.77).

These authoritative denials of Kenyon as the movement's 'Father' and the recognized roots being in Pentecostalism, provide us with substantial evidence. The most authoritative evidence breaks the invented link to metaphysical cults and reveals the mythology of McConnell, Hanegraaff and the other critics. It is one thing to expose error and heresy justly and correctly when it truly exists, the Bible gives us a clear direction to: *'Preach the word; be instant in season, out of season; reprove, rebuke, exhort with all longsuffering and doctrine'* (2 Timothy 4:2). However, to make vigorous and unyielding accusations against the 'Word of Faith' movement, that are then exposed as errors by the most authoritative voices, reveals both a serious abuse of position a gross lack of wisdom.

The Bible advises us about the type of wisdom that believers should employ: *'But the wisdom that is from above is first pure, then peaceable, gentle, and easy to be intreated, full of mercy and good fruits, without partiality, and without hypocrisy'* (James 3:17). If the critics were sincere, then surely, they would have at least employed wisdom in engaging with the movement. Rather, they have aggressively attacked the movement. The Perriman Report for example, cites John Ankerberg and John Weldon who accuse Copeland and others of 'spiritual pride,' for not receiving their offer of 'correction.' The report concludes that, 'Dialogue on the basis of criticism only, where there is no trust, is only likely to exacerbate the situation' (2003, p.232).

The 'Word of Faith' movement's supernatural heritage

Post-Apostolic period

To highlight the Biblical nature of the 'Word of Faith' movement's expectations of miracles and casting out of demons let's look briefly to the post-Apostolic early church for some testimonies showing that miracles have always been part of the church. William Young is among many who have compiled accounts of healing and deliverance within the early church. These were not as the cessationists claim, acts of God's sovereignty but rather the actions of ministers who believed they could minister deliverance and healing, according to the believers' Biblical mandate. These examples are out of step with the cessationists and much within the modern liberal church but entirely consistent with the 'Word of Faith' movement's position:

Justin Martyr (d.165) in his Dialogue with Trypho Cpt 82 believes that: 'The prophetical gifts remain with us, even to the present time.' We can continue our look into the Early church's position regarding the miraculous by reading Irenaeus (d.202) who was a pupil of Polycarp, one of the Apostle John's disciples. He wrote in Against Heresies, Book V, vi.: 'In like manner do we also hear many brethren in the church who possess prophetic gifts, and who through the Spirit speak all kinds of languages, and bring to light, for the general benefit, the hidden things of men and declare the mysteries of God, who also the apostles term spiritual.'

We go on to further consider that in Ante Nicene Fathers, Irenaeus (130AD-202AD), the Greek bishop noted for his role in combatting heresy and defining orthodoxy, wrote that: 'Those who are in truth His disciples, receiving grace from Him, do in His name perform [miracles], so as to promote the welfare of other men, according to the gift which each one has received from Him. For some do certainly and truly drive out devils, so that those who have thus been cleansed from evil spirits frequently both believe [in Christ] and join themselves to the Church. Others have foreknowledge of things to come they see visions, and utter prophetic expressions. Others still, heal the sick by laying their hands upon them, and they are made whole. Yea, moreover, as I have said, the dead even have been raised up, and remained among us for many years.... The name of our Lord Jesus Christ even now confers benefits [upon men], and cures thoroughly and effectively all who anywhere believe on Him' (Irenaeus: p.847). It is interesting that someone regarded as a senior Church Father and defender against heresy, advocated for miracles, exorcism, and healing.

Justin addresses the Roman rulers: 'When all other exorcists and sayers of charms and sellers of drugs failed, they have healed them, and still do heal, sapping the power of the demons who hold men, and driving them out' [Young 2018, p.107]. Young goes on to show that at times a simple creed was recited to minister an exorcism, as in the case of Justin to Trypho, 'every demon exorcised is conquered' [2018, p.107]. The power of this 'confession' is also a feature of the 'Word of Faith' movement. The vital component in 'confession,' is the faith for what can subsequently be done.

We can read about Tertullian who looked on exorcism as a proof that 'Christ is victorious over the Roman gods,' whom he equates with demons: 'Mock as you like, but get the demons, if you can, to join in your mocking-let them deny that Christ is coming to judge! ... Why, all the authority and power we have over them comes from our naming the Name of Christ... At our touch and breathing... they leave at our command the bodies they have entered-unwilling, distressed, and put to an open shame before your eyes' [2018, p.107]

Young goes on further to cite Irenaeus who, 'speaks of exorcisms, and more: 'Some do, really and truly, cast out demons, so that the very ones who have been cleansed from evil spirits often believe and are in the Church' [2018, pp.107,108]. He goes on to recall when 'Celsus suggests that any name is as good as another for God,' Origen gives this answer: 'The name of Jesus still takes away mental distractions from men, and daemons and diseases as well' [2018, p108].

Young mentions one of Origen's converts had the 'gift of healing to a marked extent and used it in the course of his evangelism in Pontus. About Gregory the 'Wonder Worker' we have this account: 'At daybreak, the crowd would be at the doors. Men, women, and children, those suffering from demon-possession, or other afflictions or illnesses of the body. And he in the midst would, in the power of the spirit, apportion as befitted the need of each of those who had come together. He would preach, he would join an enquiry, he would advise, he would teach, he would heal ... It was through both sight and hearing that the tokens of the Divine power shone forth upon him. For his discourses would astonish their hearing, and his wonders among the sick their sight' [2018, p108]. Given the extent of the first hand evidence of the supernatural and miraculous aspect of the Gospel throughout history, it defies both logic and faith, that people who claim to follow Jesus, could hold to a cessationist position.

Young goes on to cite Augustine's testimony of 'numerous' miracles and the first Bishop of Arbil, in Mesopotamia, who was converted in 99 A.D. 'When he saw the Syrian evangelist Addai raise a man from the dead. Mashiha-Zakha mentions this quite casually, basing his account on a written second century source. He also tells the story of a healing performed by Shahlufa, a later Bishop of Arbil, about 270' [2018, pp.109,110].

So here we can see clear evidence within the ancient church, from the post-Apostolic age, that refutes the heresy of the critical cessationists such as McConnell, MacArthur and Peters. We have abundant evidence of tongues, exorcisms and miracles. These ministries exist today within the 'Word of Faith' movement.

In addition to the early church cited above, lets briefly look at other historical figures to show the continuation within church history of supernatural events, miracles and healings.

Charles Spurgeon

Modern day critics, cessationists, and the skeptics, often have a tendency to attempt to glean authority for themselves, by aligning with noted men of history, such as Charles Spurgeon. The 'Heresy hunters' such as Peters and many of the other critics, are among this lot. However, their anti-Biblical position is diametrically opposite to Spurgeon, known as the 'Prince of Preachers,' who was certainly not a cessationist. Spurgeon was a man of faith and open to the miraculous including physical healing. Spurgeon wrote for example, 'We may know that believing prayer for the sick is far more likely to be followed by restoration than anything else in the world' [Spurgeon, 2018]. There are many testimonies of healing from Spurgeon's life, it formed a definite part of his ministry as we can see from the following testimony: 'Spurgeon collected and read books on divine healing. He often was called to pray for his parishioners in the midst of their sicknesses. Many remarkable healings occurred. It is said that over the course of his ministry that thousands of people had received prayer from him and had been healed. He was moved, not by intellectual assent to God's healing ability, but simply by a deep sense of compassion and faith in God's answering of prayer. In 1855, Spurgeon prayed for a man who had been critically ill with fever. He attended the church meeting that night and told his acquaintances "Mr. Spurgeon prayed with me this morning. I have been divinely healed." In that same time period, a man with partial paralysis was prayed for by Spurgeon and the limp he had for years disappeared. Spurgeon prayed for a man crippled by rheumatism one morning. He felt better immediately and asked Spurgeon to return that evening to pray again. When Spurgeon returned the man met him at the door and told him "The Lord is performing His promises and has answered your prayer." The man was completely well.' [Healing and Revival: 2019].

Spurgeon's Calvinistic theology was very different to the cessationist Calvinists within much of the modern church. Critics such as John MacArthur, Justin Peters and many of the others, embrace Spurgeon for their Calvinistic ends but they deny his true ministry and its supernatural emphasis. In truth, Spurgeon was far closer to the 'Word of Faith' movement, his miraculous emphasis is precisely what the 'Word of Faith' movement have taught and why there have been so many similarly tremendous testimonies within the movement.

John Wesley

In the previous century to Spurgeon, John Wesley the Methodist leader was involved in many supernatural healings. Here is an account from his own diary of one on Christmas Day 1742: 'The Physician told me he could do no more; Mr. Meyrick could not live over the night. I went up and found them all crying about him; his legs being cold, and (as it seemed) dead already. We all kneeled down and called upon God with strong cries and tears. He opened his eyes, and called for me; and, from that hour, he continued to recover his strength, till he was restored to perfect health' (Jennings 2005, pp. 49,50).

John Wesley emphatically and specifically refutes the cessationist position which so many of the critics of the 'Word of Faith' movement have adopted, he writes: 'I do not recollect any scripture wherein we are taught that miracles were to be confined within the limits either of the apostolic or the Cyprianic age; or of any period of time, longer or shorter, even till the restitution of all things. I have not observed, either in the Old Testament or the New, any intimation at all of this kind' (2005, pp.196). Wesley's words even today, expose the radical sceptics such as MacArthur and Peters. Their extreme denial of much within the New Testament, has historically, and will continue to be, unacceptable to Bible believing Christians.

Daniel Jennings has written an entire book from the diaries of John Wesley in which there are numerous testimonies of supernatural events, miracles, and healings. Wesley's position was clear, Jennings writes, 'For Wesley, any person possessing true saving faith could experience these miracles: It was not one faith by which St. Paul was saved, another by which he wrought miracles. Even at this day in every believer faith has a latent miraculous power; (every effect of prayer being really miraculous;) although in many, both because of their own littleness of faith, and because the world is unworthy, that power is not exerted' (2005 pp.196,197).

The 'Word of Faith' movement has been heavily criticized for connecting the receiving of physical healing with faith. However, what is clear is that Wesley cited in the quote above, suggests that 'littleness of faith' is one of the reasons for people not releasing the power that is latent within them. We can also show that Luther and Spurgeon also linked faith with receiving from God. Clearly these historical leaders of the church based the foundation of their ministry similarly to the 'Word of Faith' movement, on the Bible, rather than western theological traditions. The Bible itself is repeatedly very clear, *'And whatever things you ask in prayer, believing, you will receive'* (Matthew 21:22).

Martin Luther

Martin Luther the German theologian known for his Ninety-five Theses of 1517 and the Reformation which followed, had a strong desire to live according to Biblical truth. We can see that faith in the life of Luther, and I recall here two supernatural healings out of many, that were part of his ministry. The first happened when he received word that his friend and colleague, Frederick Myconius, lay dying in the last stages of tuberculosis. 'When Luther read this report, a supernatural and bold faith rose up in his heart. He then penned a letter to Myconius in which he said, "I command you in the Name of God to live because I still have need of you in the work of reforming the Church. The Lord will never let me hear that you are dead but will permit you to survive me. For this I am praying, this is my will, and may my will be done because I seek only to glorify the Name of God." Myconius said that when he read the letter it seemed as though he heard Christ say, "Lazarus, come forth!" Luther's words were fulfilled. Myconius was healed and outlived Luther by two months' [Hyatt, 2017]. This account has the hallmarks of bold faith, of the kind promoted by the 'Word of Faith' movement, and an understanding of our position of authority to command things according to our will. This is what Jesus taught believers to do: *'For verily I say unto you, That whosoever shall say unto this mountain, Be thou removed, and be thou cast into the sea; and shall not doubt in his heart, but shall believe that those things which he saith shall come to pass; he shall have whatsoever he saith'* (Mark 11:23). Notice, *'he shall have whatsoever he saith.'* This is a 'Word of Faith' type ministry, clearly exhibited in the life of Martin Luther.

There was another occasion when Luther's colleague Philip Melanchthon became extremely ill and was very close to death. The testimony of this miracle happened as 'Luther is said to have fervently prayed, using all the relevant promises he could repeat from Scripture. As he prayed, a supernatural faith rose up in his heart. He then turned, and taking Melanchthon by the hand, said, "Be of good courage, Philip, you shall not die." Melanchthon immediately revived and soon regained his health. He later said, "I should have been a dead man had I not been recalled from death itself by the coming of Luther." [Hyatt, 2017]. Again, what we can evidence is the supernatural expectation and application of Bible-based faith. Luther clearly did what the 'Word of Faith' movement has taught for many years, he *'spoke those things which be not as though they were'* (Romans 4:17b). This is another area where the critics of the 'Word of Faith' movement have attacked, they deny the power of our words.

Word of Faith

The 'Word of Faith' movement is of a supernatural Bible-based heritage. The movement continues in a vast line of people of faith throughout the centuries. From the Bible itself, into the early church, right through to Luther, Wesley, Spurgeon, Pentecostalism, and Charismatic believers of today. The movement has developed a theology which has helped to further understand our authority as believers, our potential as Kingdom ambassadors, our understanding and application of faith, the power of words, and many other Biblical doctrines.

Kenneth Hagin's influences

While Hagin was clearly influenced by Kenyon, what has been understated by the critics is the influence of the Pentecostal, Holiness, and Revivalist streams. Again, the understating of these influences helped towards building their mythology. The Perriman Report insightfully cites the noted Pentecostal Evangelist F.F. Bosworth whose book 'Christ the healer' contains most of what the 'Word of Faith' movement teach regarding faith and healing. It goes on to explain that Bosworth taught that it was essential to have faith in healing before a person would receive healing (2003, p.63). Hagin also references some of the pre-Pentecostal influences on his theology. For example, during the message, 'Why Do People Fall Under the Power,' Hagin comments, 'Did you ever read after John Wesley? I began to read John Wesley's writings first way back in 1938. John Wesley, of course, is the father, you know, of Methodism...(and) it became quite a frequent thing in his services for people, sometimes hundreds of them, to fall under the power.... Did you ever read the autobiography of Charles G. Finney? I have more than once. It has blessed me immeasurably.... George Whitefield, who was a co-laborer with John Wesley actually, came over here to America, and it is a historical fact.... Did you ever read after Peter Cartwright? The Wesley-Methodist preacher, you know, I read his autobiography' (Hagin, 1976). Hagin shows that these recognizable Christian leaders of the Methodist, Pentecostal and Holiness traditions, were his inspiration. Much of this understanding would be reflected in Hagin's subsequent teaching, again showing clear similarities with early Pentecostalism.

Charles Farah, who was McConnell's professor at Oral Roberts University, identifies that the real roots of the 'Word of Faith' movement's theology are found in the teaching of the nineteenth-century revivalist Charles Finney. As mentioned previously Hagin has confirmed the influence of Finney. Finney defines faith as that which always obtains the blessing it seeks, he teaches: 'I am speaking now of the kind of faith that ensures the blessing' (1993, p.76). Again, this assurance of faith was taught very clearly in Hagin's ministry.

In conclusion, the evidence shows that the 'Word of Faith' movement and the teaching of Hagin has been significantly impacted by early Pentecostalism. Smith Wigglesworth for example, an early Pentecostal minister and often known as the 'Apostle of faith,' teaches, 'It is a blessed thing to learn that God's word can never fail' (1924, p.30). This phrase and theological perspective by Wigglesworth were echoed by Hagin in his 1996 book, 'God's Word: A Never Failing Remedy.' As we have already shown, Hagin himself was ordained as an Assemblies of God minister in 1967. Wigglesworth continues, 'I am not moved by what I see. I am moved only by what I believe. No man considers how he feels if he believes. The man who believes God, has it' (1924, p.30). It is interesting to note that Kenneth Copeland's Theme song for the television broadcast called The Way, also includes the words, 'I am not moved by what I see.' The 'Word of Faith' movement is not moved by feelings but rather by faith.

What Wigglesworth and Copeland are saying here, has been classified as 'Sensory denial through positive confession.' A. B. Simpson, similarly, wrote, 'We believe that God is healing before any evidence is given' (Barron, p.60). We can see that Hagin was clearly influenced by this position and cites Wigglesworth in his highly influential book, 'The Believer's Authority,' he writes: 'I'm not moved by what I feel. I'm moved only by what I believe. So stand your ground' (1984, p.24).

What is clear is that Hagin was influenced by established Christian leaders and there were indeed no metaphysical influences impacting on his theology. Clearly, a plethora of Christian history and theology has been overlooked by the critics, a significant blunder, given the force of their claims.

Chapter 5
McConnell's Mythology

McConnell's mythology of the 'Word of Faith' movement:

The view which holds to the idea that Kenyon was the founding father of the 'Word of Faith' movement, was popularized by McConnell in his master's thesis at Oral Roberts University in 1982. Bowman has noted two earlier references in 1980 that claimed a link between the 'Word of Faith' movement and the metaphysical cults, but it was McConnell's thesis which brought the debate to wider recognition (2001, p.231). Even before 1980 in 1979, the debate about the origins of the movement was hinted at, when McConnell's professor at Oral Roberts University Charles Farah, published a critique of the 'Word of Faith' movement entitled, 'From the Pinnacle of the Temple' (Perriman 2003, p.13). The book asked questions about the nature of Christian faith and the possibility of Christian presumptions regarding expectations of physical healings. However, McConnell's thesis went further than Farah's book and concluded that the 'Word of Faith' movement was cultic because of its metaphysical origins (1988, pp.185-186). This was the conclusion of McConnell's work, and given the plethora of evidence available, as such, it constitutes mythology. This mythology has inspired many of the subsequent critics.

According to Bowman, McConnell's thesis was 'startling' in that he claimed the movement did not originate within Pentecostalism but rather it was rooted in Kenyon's 'New Thought' metaphysics (2001, p.9). Bowman's point that McConnell's thesis was 'startling' is worth noting because, until McConnell's mythology, the movement was generally accepted without question. McIntyre responds to McConnell's metaphysical claims regarding Kenyon, by correctly asserting that Kenyon was influenced by the Faith-Cure Christian evangelical movement which started around 1873 and was absorbed into the Pentecostal movement in the early 1900's (1997, pp.60, 226).

McConnell's other observation has been that Hagin has significantly plagiarized the writings of Kenyon (1988, pp.6-13). McConnell has taken care to highlight the extent of the plagiarizing by devoting four pages of his book, to compare large portions of Kenyon's work with Hagin's. Often the two works seem to read in an exact word for word parallel. Without a context, it might appear on the surface that Hagin had been involved in plagiarism. However, DeArteaga cites various examples of when Hagin did acknowledge Kenyon and he, like most, regards Hagin as having a good deal of personal integrity. Consequently, he considers that any 'plagiarism' accusation ought to be understood as taking place during a time when the informal 'borrowing' of ideas was normative for ministers of his background (2003, p.244). DeArteaga also notes that Hagin's books and pamphlets were often simply transcriptions of Hagin's sermons and tapes. He goes on to suggest that because Hagin, who had a photographic memory, preached these books into existence he could not be expected to cite his sources. Consequently, he claims that Kenyon's ideas were transcribed without reference onto the pages of Hagin's books. Furthermore, Hagin's photographic memory, might in DeArteaga's opinion, account for the exact wording from Kenyon within Hagin's work.

What McConnell and the other critics also overlook, is that when someone is involved in plagiarizing, they don't often copy large paragraphs, they limit copying to a sentence or a point. This clearly shows that Hagin's intentions were not to plagiarize, neither were they lacking in integrity.

Furthermore, in what should end any issue altogether, Kenyon's own publishing company writes the following: 'We consider Kenneth E. Hagin to be a great man of God. If E.W. Kenyon were here today, he and Hagin would probably be good friends. And from his vantage point in heaven, Kenyon is probably delighted that Kenneth E. Hagin has been so successful in getting the message of faith, so dear to Kenyon's heart, out to so many in the world in this generation. If Kenyon himself wouldn't be bothered about it all, why should anyone else?' [Kenyons, 2018].

The same publishing company has also defended Hagin using three separate points, in summary, form here:

1)   Someone transcribes the taped messages, and then they are edited and put into book form. Those who are preachers understand that

it is impossible to stop and credit everyone who influenced your message while you are preaching.
2) A second thought that bears on this subject: All of those ministers who worked with Kenyon used his terminology and catchy phrases. It would be hard to imagine him being offended by this.
3) A third point: He [Hagin] credits Kenyon both on the tapes and in the introduction to the book. He worked, through his editor, with Kenyon's Gospel Publishing Society and had the complete approval of Ruth Kenyon Housworth (Kenyon's late daughter) for the book when it went to print. Hagin's ministry has always maintained a good relationship with Kenyon's Gospel Publishing Society. One of Kenyon's books is used in the curriculum at Hagin's Rhema Bible Training Center' [Kenyon's, 2018].

Given that Kenyon's own publisher has no issue with Hagin's lack of specific reference citations, why does McConnell make such a point out of it? It appears that McConnell was keen to try anything to undermine Hagin and perpetuate the mythology of the link to the metaphysical cults. Again, the essential points above seem to have been entirely overlooked by 'Word of Faith' critics and this puts into question their ability to extract a fair, balanced, and well-researched appraisal.

The Perriman Report has observed that within the vast number of quasi-Christian groups in the nineteenth century two general categories emerged. On the one hand were eschatological cults such as Mormonism, Jehovah's Witnesses, and the Worldwide Church of God, etc. In the other category, were the a-historical or 'Gnostic' cults, which had an emphasis on the powers of the 'mental and spiritual worlds' (2003, p.67). It was this latter category that promoted self-realization and the ability to succeed, often labeled as 'New Thought Metaphysics,' (2003, pp.67-68) which McConnell has attempted to connect with Kenyon (1988, p.92).

McConnell created the mythology that Kenyon was cultic, metaphysical and the father of the 'Word of Faith' movement. This was an attempt to discredit the 'Word of Faith' movement by association. Kenyon wasn't the movement's father, neither was he cultic or metaphysical. The attempt to link the movement to the metaphysical cults is both historically inaccurate and dangerously misleading.

Steven Lyn Evans

McConnell's critique of Kenyan's ministry and influences:

Unitarianism

At one point in his life, Kenyon regularly attended services at the Unitarian church of Minot J. Savage in Boston. The Perriman Report cites McConnell's opinion that this is 'suspicious' for two reasons. Firstly, Unitarianism with their central belief in the goodness of mankind opposed many orthodox Christian doctrines such as the Trinity, Divinity of Jesus, the Atonement, the Fall, and eternal punishment (Cross & Livingstone 2005, p.1671). Secondly, Kenyon had varied doctrinal influences, and these have been referred to by McConnell and cited within the Perriman Report which suggests that 'falling out of love with orthodoxy in the nineteenth century, was a convenient staging post on the way to Transcendentalism and New Thought' (2003, p.71). What these points overlook, is the history that DeArteaga has pointed out, that Kenyon's spiritual breakthrough came from a recognized Christian church, it did not take place in the Unitarianism propagated by Minot J. Savage, but rather during a visit to a Baptist Church led by A.J. Gordon (2003, p.75). McConnell seems to have ignored this rather crucial evidence as it offers clear and relevant historical facts, which undermine his mythological claims.

Furthermore, any claim that Kenyon had adopted the unorthodox teachings of Unitarianism would need to explain Kenyon's explicit and repeated objections to that movement (McIntyre 1997, p.304; DeArteaga 1992, pp.214-215). McIntyre goes on to emphasize this point by citing McConnell's quote of Kenyon's severe critique of Unitarianism in which, Kenyon observes that 'They do not believe that Jesus died for our sins, but that He died a martyr. They do not believe He had a literal resurrection, a physical resurrection, but as one puts it, "a metaphysical resurrection" whatever that means' (1988, p.43). There are further significant references within Kenyon's own work that explicitly refute the Unitarian position. Nevertheless, McConnell contests that many within the faith movement issue disclaimers when their doctrines are similar to cults (1988, p.43). However, in saying this, McConnell is refusing to accept the objective evidence, even when it is historically or theologically factual, if it refutes his position. The Perriman Report offers another insightful and key observation on this issue: 'Similarities do not necessarily indicate dependence, and dependence does not always indicate a common purpose.' (2003, p.76).

Even if we ignored the evidence and considered the claims of a Unitarian influence were correct, it has been noted by DeArteaga and agreed within the Perriman Report that we should warn against the 'genetic fallacy of rejecting an idea because of where it comes from rather than disproving the argument' (2003, p.76; 1992, p.246).

Metaphysics

McConnell claims that Kenyon is the father of the 'Word of Faith' movement because conceptual parallels seem to exist between the 'Word of Faith' movement, the teachings of Kenyon, and the metaphysical cults (Perriman 2003, p.73). For example, Kenyon believed that sickness was spiritual, therefore, any cure needed to be found within the spiritual realm. McConnell consequently claimed that Kenyon's doctrine appears very similar to the metaphysical cults, who also believed that diseases and subsequent cures were spiritual in origin (1988, p.150). Metaphysics insists that the spiritual realm always governs the physical and that healing can only be attained through the spiritual realm (McIntyre 1997, p.212). However, for Kenyon, whilst the antidote to sickness was spiritual, it was not metaphysical and mind centered, it was rather centered on the redemptive work of Christ Jesus, through the atonement. McIntyre explains, that even if there were metaphysical influences on Kenyon, they became passé through both his consistent rejection of metaphysical doctrines (1997, p.228) and his references to Christ Jesus as the source of healing rather than the human mind (1997, p.225). Kenyon makes this distinction very clear in his own words: 'It is not mental as Christian Science and other metaphysical teachers claim...when God heals He heals through the spirit' (Kenyon 1943, p.90). In one of several messages from 1929, Kenyon points out that some follow, 'another Jesus,' he explains: 'Jesus is a metaphysical, philosophical creation to them, — to me he is the very Son of God conceived of the Holy Spirit, born of the Virgin, lived, suffered, died and paid the penalty of our transgressions; met Satan in mortal combat in the lower regions, conquered him, stripped him of his power and authority, and rose from the dead with the keys of death and Hades in His hands' [Kenyon's, 2018]. With such a clear differentiation from Kenyon's own teaching towards the metaphysical cults, it is difficult to understand how the critics could possibly defend their claims. Therefore, any apparent link, from Kenyon to the metaphysical cults is clearly unfounded. Claims of a connection offer only a surface appraisal of the evidence. The critics have used this veneer to promote mythology and doubt against the movement.

McIntyre observes that by 1892 Kenyon had slipped into a brief agnostic period and consequently enrolled at the Emerson College of Oratory to help rekindle his ambitions to become an actor (1997, p.16). Charles Emerson, the founder of this college, is considered by McConnell as being typical of many intellectuals during that period of the late nineteenth century, who were journeying from traditional theism to metaphysics (Perriman 2003, p.73). McConnell believes Emerson was a 'vigorous propagandist' and would have influenced Kenyon with his 'erratic religious thinking' (2003, p.72). Emerson himself, according to McConnell was a religious eclectic who readily accepted the influence of an array of movements such as Transcendentalism, Social Darwinism, New Thought Metaphysics, Platonism, and Swedenborgianism to name but a few (1988, p.35). Furthermore, Emerson eventually converted to the metaphysical teachings of Christian Science in 1903 (McConnell 1988, p. 37). However, concerning the Emerson College of Oratory, its influence over Kenyon has repeatedly been questioned (Bowman 2001, p.65; McIntyre 1997, pp.16-18). McIntyre has shown that Emerson the man, in stark contrast to the figure depicted by McConnell, at the time of Kenyon's studentship was highly regarded by significant Holiness and Faith-Cure movement leaders such as Cullis and also the Methodist church (McIntyre 1997, p.17). Furthermore, it is interesting to note that the Perriman Report has suggested in its critique of McConnell that, 'the influence of Emerson College on Kenyon's thinking may have been exaggerated' and perhaps most surprisingly the report concludes that if anything, the college might have been 'too conservative' for Kenyan at that time (2003, p.75). This criticism of McConnell from the Perriman Report is highly significant in its strong consideration of 'exaggerating.' Also, the lack of historical context in the timeline of the Emerson College's influences, is a significant oversight by McConnell.

Furthermore, DeArteaga suggests that Kenyon's clear and wide-ranging associations are to be found within traditional Pentecostalism, rather than the schools of New Thought and metaphysics. (Perriman 2003, p.75). The Perriman Report quotes DeArteaga's assertion that Kenyon, 'poured away the heretical bathwater of New Thought metaphysics but kept the baby of faith in God's abundant provision' (Perriman 2003, p.74).

McConnell's views regarding the negative influence of the Emerson experience on Kenyon seem to omit specific readily available facts. For example, Emerson College at the time of Kenyon's studentship was also a training college for Christian ministry and a highly respected center of education, i.e., from 1890-1920 Emerson College was recognized as one of America's most prominent in the field of vocal expression (McIntyre

1997, p.16). Also, Kenyon's ordination as Free Will Baptist minister on January 17th, 1894 (McIntyre 1997, p.26) reveals that shortly after leaving Emerson, he was aligned with the conventional expectations of the Baptist denomination to the full satisfaction of the ordaining body.

The Perriman Report also cited the metaphysical issue and summarizes the position well, in the observation that: 'The central belief was that a person's material and spiritual circumstances may be changed by the power of the mind' (2003, p.68). Given the potential influence of scientific advances in the area of quantum physics during Kenyon's formative years, it would be presumptuous to ignore the possibility that his thinking was not influenced to some degree by the modern discoveries of his day. DeArteaga has noted for example, that Max Planck (1848-1947) the discoverer of quantum physics showed that the mind had the power to influence matter by observation and this 'had a mathematical expression in the central equation of quantum physics' (2001, p.146). Nevertheless, McIntyre points out that 'when Kenyon said the source of sickness was spiritual, not physical, he was referring to sickness's roots in Satan, sin, and the 'Fall' (1997, p.212). Therefore, any similarities between Kenyon's understanding of spiritual, and the metaphysical understanding of spiritual can once again only be understood from a somewhat shallow perspective, without regard to the intent of meaning, or context. For example, when Hanegraaff cites 'Word of Faith' preacher Jerry Savelle, "When the Devil tries to put a symptom of sickness or disease on my body, I absolutely refuse to accept it" (1993, p.243), McConnell uses such examples to argue the metaphysical connection because a fundamental tenet of this belief is the denial of the reality of sickness (McIntyre 1997, p.309). However, the significant difference between the metaphysical cults and the 'Word of Faith' movement in this area is expressed by Savelle's subsequent explanation that his views are centered on faith in Jesus and Biblical promises of healing, not on mental ascent (1993, p.243). Hanegraaff has again, not cited the quote within its fuller context and explanation. The critics seem pathologically unable to accept this vital and clear distinction, they appear to be content to disregard the movements acknowledgment of Jesus Christ as the healer, to perpetuate their mythology. The current 'Word of Faith' position is similar to Kenyon's and for that matter many other Christians, it is not qualified by the mind, or in self-knowledge as in metaphysics, but rather by exercising faith in Jesus Christ and Biblical promises of healing.

Bowman, who according to the Perriman Report offers the most balanced research on the 'Word of Faith' movement concluded emphatically: 'Kenyon never ministered in metaphysical contexts, never modeled his ministry institution on metaphysical ones, and was never received by the metaphysical community. By contrast, all three of these things are true of Kenyon's connections with the evangelical faith-cure and early Pentecostal movements (2001, pp.66,67).

Another 'Word of Faith' type doctrine was promoted by Fillmore (1854-1948) and Trine (1866-1958) who was a classmate of Kenyon's at Emerson College (McIntyre 1997, p.15), Trine claimed that faith in God would necessarily result in personal prosperity (Perriman 2003, p.69). McConnell cites the potential influence of the highly popular metaphysical teachings of Trine regarding 'personal prosperity' over Kenyon (1988, pp.40-42). However, any similarities between the modern 'Word of Faith' movement and Trine's doctrine of personal prosperity, could not in all probability be linked through Kenyon, because as the Perriman Report has observed, Kenyon was not at all focused-on material prosperity (2003, p.73). Here is another reason why Kenyon could not be regarded as the father of the 'Word of Faith' movement.

DeArteaga's observation along with the Perriman Report highlights significant issues within McConnell's thesis. For example, if Kenyon was guilty as McConnell has suggested of syncretism, with his famous colleague Trine regarding 'personal prosperity,' then why does the objective evidence point to a position that is clearly opposite to this? The Perriman Report, DeArteaga, McIntyre, and others are clear in their views that Kenyon was not particularly interested in material prosperity (Perriman 2003, pp.73-74). Once again, the critics have woven together mythology. They have succeeded in repeatedly twisting the facts and ignoring the available evidence.

Syncretism

McConnell believes that regardless of Kenyon's frequent critiques of the metaphysical cults he had assimilated a great deal of their thinking and terminology and was, therefore, a classic example of religious syncretism (1988, p.48). McConnell concludes that 'although his intent was to help the church, Kenyon's syncretism of cultic ideas resulted in a strange blend of evangelical fundamentalism and New Thought metaphysics, in his attempt to correct one error, Kenyon created another' (1988, p.48). In response, DeArteaga has suggested that Kenyon was not guilty of syncretism with the metaphysical cults, but rather as the Perriman Report suggests, he modified the idealism of New Thought beliefs and used them to offer a contemporary exposure of the failings of both the cessationists and materialist consensus, which was prevailing in the church (Perriman 2003, p.74). This appraisal is both consistent with Kenyon's own words and the overall emphasis of his ministry.

DeArteaga accuses McConnell's perspective of coming from a cessationist, anti-charismatic bias. He also suggests in his response to McConnell that Kenyon's arguments were used to strengthen the orthodox faith against what he regards as the corrosive effect of higher criticism (Perriman 2003, p.74). Therefore, rather than interpreting Kenyon's doctrines as a watered-down syncretistic gospel suggested by McConnell, DeArteaga has offered a diametrically opposite opinion, in favor of Kenyon's orthodoxy.

Since 'The Enlightenment,' the teaching of Critical Theory developed and took the form of Higher and Lower Criticism within the church. This has often led to unorthodox and at times bizarre positions being claimed from within the 'church.' We could consider examples of liberal positions within many denominations. Clearly, the 'Word of Faith' movement and Kenyon, have stood up for Biblical views. DeArteaga has been correct to suggest that Kenyon's position has contributed towards the orthodox Christian Biblical position.

Kenyon is not the Father of the 'Word of Faith' movement

McConnell's mythology links metaphysical cults to Kenyon, and this allows him to categorize the 'Word of Faith' movement as 'cultic.' However, for McConnell to have claimed this, a large amount of evidence would have had to have been ignored, to the degree that, McConnell's mythology of Kenyon bears very little resemblance to the evidential reality.

It was not until Hagin that the beginnings of the 'Word of Faith' movement can be seen as existing. As has been noted by the Perriman Report, the movement originated after the Second World War (2003, p. xviii), and grew in parallel with the ministry of Hagin rather than Kenyon who died in 1948. The movement's largest official network the 'International Convention of Faith Ministries,' was founded in 1979 by Hagin and a group of his colleagues, over thirty years after Kenyon's death. It is, therefore, clearly wrong to claim Kenyon as the movement's father. To view Kenyon as a significant and influencing voice would be accurate but anything more is an exaggeration. Nevertheless, its suited McConnell's mythology and critical aims to attempt to make Kenyon the movement's father.

Hagin orchestrated and taught many 'Word of Faith' students from his college campus in Broken Arrow, Oklahoma. Bowman considers this college to be the movement's principal educational base (2001, p.8). Consequently, Bowman has been correct in his assertion that Hagin, rather than Kenyon, is the father of the 'Word of Faith' movement (2001, p.36). Furthermore, it has been noted by the Perriman Report that the 'Word of Faith' movement itself has often not recognized Kenyon's influence (2003, p.70), rather, they affectionately refer to Hagin as the 'Daddy' of the movement (2003, p.1).

As previously mentioned, McIntyre has observed that Kenyon was not at all focused-on material prosperity. As a Free Will Baptist minister, Kenyon had felt the conviction to refuse his salary and enter into a 'life of trust' (1997, pp.96-97). This emphasis would not necessarily be shared by the 'Word of Faith' movement. Many within the movement, for example, have embraced a prosperity emphasis which was developed through Hagin and then Copeland and was expressed in Copeland's 1974 book, 'The Laws of Prosperity.'

There is a similarity of integrity though, when Kenyon resigned from the Free Will Baptist denomination for example, because of his intense desire for financial integrity. As McIntyre suggests, 'he insisted that his Free Will Baptist Church get out of debt and stop using manipulative methods to raise his salary' (1997, p.63). This refusal of debt and manipulative methodology has also been explicitly taught by Kenneth Copeland (2011, pp.342,342).

Kenyon had a keen desire to be free from even the slightest emphasis of what might be regarded as financial manipulation and irregularities. Consequently, Kenyon discontinued the 'collection' habits of a church from actively passing buckets around the congregation, to the provision of a simple and non-threatening box by the door (McIntyre 1997, p.97). The Perriman Report has also observed Kenyon's emphasis within this area and concluded that 'Kenyon was perhaps too much of a mystic and a romantic to be an unabashed advocate of material prosperity' (2003, p.73). It is clear that Kenyon's beliefs and teaching regarding financial prosperity differed in varying degrees, to the 'Word of Faith' movement, which the Perriman Report has correctly suggested advocates for 'material prosperity' (2003, p.14). We should also remember that the 'Word of Faith' movement has recognized that prosperity is found in the realms of the spirit, soul (mind, will and emotions) and physical body and is not merely about financial provision.

Bowman has noted other significant areas of doctrinal difference between Kenyon and the 'Word of Faith' doctrines (2001, pp.126, 125) but the movement's prosperity ethos contrasts strikingly to Kenyon's ministry, which seemed to have adopted an almost ascetic approach at times. For example, within Kenyon's Bethel Bible Institute he ordered that 'no teacher or head of Department or anyone however connected with the institution shall ever receive a salary' (Perriman 2003, p.71). Kenyon's has a lack of emphasis regarding financial prosperity, and the 'Word of Faith' movement has a strong emphasis (Perriman 2003, p.235). Once again, the claims of McConnell and the other critics, suggesting Kenyon is the 'Word of Faith' movement's father, exaggerate Kenyon's influence.

In conclusion, once it is accepted that Kenyon clearly isn't the father of the movement and it is recognized that Hagin is, then the invented link to the metaphysical cults is broken, and McConnell, Hanegraaff, Peters and the other critics' entire mythology is exposed. This conclusion is verified by Bowman who has taken care to point out the widespread acknowledgment that 'Hagin had no significant contact with the metaphysical cults' (2001, p.48). Once the mythology of a link between the 'Word of Faith' movement and the metaphysical cults is exposed, the way is open to returning to the overriding pre-McConnell view, shared by Bowman and the Perriman Report, that the 'Word of Faith' movement has roots in Pentecostalism (2001, p.7; 2003, p.77). This is very significant because a movement with established Pentecostal roots has more of an open doorway for fellowship with the broader Christian church without suspicion and prejudice. This fellowship has been hindered because of the critics' mythology and the accusation of a connection to the metaphysical cults.

Chapter 6

The centrality and commonality of the atonement

Introduction

As we have noted previously, the Perriman Report suggests that the critics of the 'Word of Faith' movement claim that the movement 'diverges from sound doctrine at certain key points, most notably in its understanding of the atonement' (2003, p.14). The report also suggests that the debate regarding the orthodoxy and roots of the 'Word of Faith' movement 'has been marred by misrepresentation, polarization, and invective' (2003, p.15). In other words, the truth has been hindered by the critical voices. Therefore, in analyzing the atonement we will establish the orthodoxy of the 'Word of Faith' movement's doctrine through comparison to a leading recognized historical authority on the subject, Bishop Gustaf Aulén (1879-1978).

It will be shown that there are three main historical periods of development within Atonement doctrines. The first period being the 'Classical' or Ransom motif. Next 'Penal Substitution' or 'Satisfaction' doctrine, and finally 'Protestant Orthodoxy' or 'Exchange' doctrine. In effect, a theological experiment is being employed, which will search for clear answers regarding the orthodoxy of the 'Word of Faith' movement.

Issues relating to an assessment of the movement

Firstly, perhaps it is not surprising that there have been significant problems in establishing true and balanced appraisals of the movement (Perriman 2003, p.1). This would be the case for most movements within the church. Anglicanism for example, it would be difficult to establish a continuity of teaching given that on one side there is the Charismatic arm, and on the other side High Church Liturgy. Bowman has noted, not all of the 'Word of Faith' teachers seem to share all of the doctrines (2001, p.30). Bowman's observation was in response to arguments presented by Hanegraaff, which he considered as being too simplistic, in that they often implied the 'Word of Faith' movement has one clear set of doctrines. Hanegraaff typifies the critics and instead of engaging with balance shows a pathological desire to attack the movement. Commenting on his work it has been observed that, 'behind its numerous citations and quotations lays a profound methodological error, the assumption that listing the worst errors of a movement is a truthful representation of that movement' (DeArteaga 1992, p.269). This supports the accusation that the criticisms of the movement are often nothing more than mere characterizations.

Within the movement, as is the case with any other movement, there is a mixture of emphasis within the doctrines. In relation to this, Bowman has observed that a progression exists in which, 'Hagin takes matters to a more extreme point than E. W. Kenyon did, and in turn, Kenneth Copeland has taken ideas and pushed them further than Hagin (2001, p.225). This is not a criticism but an observation. Jesus Christ offered the most extreme teachings known to mankind, developing ideas further can at times, be likened to developing a greater understanding or revelation. Progressing further in Christian discipleship for example and *'from faith to faith'* (Romans 1:17). It is worth noting that throughout the history of the church, Christian leaders have always taught the Biblical truth, which within their initial theological context, often appeared at first to be extreme. Martin Luther for example, when he first taught the Biblical notion of 'Grace' was regarded as extreme because this Biblical doctrine and emphasis, had been largely ignored by the church. Today, we can see that a similar thing has happened via the teaching ministries of the 'Word of Faith' movement. This movement has been used to enthuse and inspire people towards Biblical faith and a sure foundation.

The Perriman Report takes care to suggest that critics of the 'Word of Faith' movement tend to be biased in their use of the limited historical and biographical material which has, 'frequently been assembled for the purpose of discrediting the movement' (2003, p.1). A polarization has taken place in which critical arguments have gravitated towards that, which on the surface might appear unorthodox, rather than working to find a balanced understanding and appraisal.

The Perriman Report has also suggested there is a lack of resource information pertaining to the doctrines of belief within the 'Word of Faith' movement. In addition, it goes on to observe that there is also a lack of clear consensus among the 'Word of Faith' preachers themselves (Perriman 2003, p.1). However, all movements have a certain scope regarding emphasis on doctrines that are not essential and the 'Word of Faith' movement is no different. It should also be noted that the ICFM, which can be considered as perhaps the main historical organization of the 'Word of Faith' movement, offers a specific list of its beliefs. Many of the original founders of the 'Word of Faith' movement are still within the membership and that includes the most senior founder member, Kenneth Copeland. Therefore, claims that the movement's doctrines are difficult to find are not entirely accurate, certainly the main ones can be found easily via the ICFM.

What is perhaps more the point is that some teachings, which were perhaps not essential and might have been open to various interpretations, have not been emphasized by the movement.

Why test the atonement doctrine?

The Atonement has been described by Morris as the central doctrine of the Christian church (Morris 1993, p.54). Hanegraaff has also recognized that 'the atonement is crucial to the historical Christian faith' (1993, p152). Therefore, in evaluating the 'Word of Faith' movement, an examination of the teaching on the atonement is highly beneficial in helping to establish historically recognizable Christian doctrines.

The Perriman Report commissioned by the Evangelical Alliance has commented that critics of the 'Word of Faith' movement suggest that the movement strays from orthodoxy on key points of doctrine and notably on the atonement (2003, p.14). Bowman has noted that McConnell, the inventor of the critics' mythology, has denied discrediting the movement merely on its association with Kenyon (Bowman 2001, p.25). McConnell points rather, towards the twofold accusation that the movement 'is cultic not just because of where it comes from, but also because of what it teaches' (1988, pp.51-52).

McConnell's 1982 Masters' thesis, to a large degree centered on the link from the then current teachings of Hagin, to Kenyon, and from Kenyon he attempted to draw parallels with the metaphysical cults. This was his attempt to discredit the foundations of the 'Word of Faith' movement and create a mythology (1988, pp.15-28). Most of the subsequent criticisms of the 'Word of Faith' movement follow McConnell's pattern and center on the mythology of Kenyon's supposed connection with the metaphysical cults. This claim has already been shown to be inaccurate within this work, but we will soon address further issues that discredit McConnell's mythology.

Probably the most publicized follower of this thesis is Hanegraaff, who suggests that what separates Christianity from cults is unity on essential matters such as the atonement, Hanegraaff quotes Augustine to emphasize his point (1993, p.47). However, here we can see both irony and weaknesses within the argument because Kenyon's atonement motifs are often theologically 'Classical' and therefore very similar to Augustine's. This connection has not been recognized by Hanegraaff. Kenyon in part shares a unity of atonement motif with Augustine, but Hanegraaff's atonement beliefs are not in unity with either of them. Hanegraaff refutes the 'Classical' atonement ransom motif for example (1993, p.153) and suggests instead the more recent 'Protestant Orthodox' position (1993, pp.152-153). Hanegraaff doesn't make any mention of the historical 'Classical' atonement doctrine. He, like McConnell, offers little insight into the history of the atonement and this might explain why they have been so inaccurate in their conclusions of Kenyan and the 'Word of Faith' movement. This lack of historical awareness by Hanegraaff has been observed by DeArteaga, he has suggested that Hanegraaff's arguments lack 'a broad Christian historical perspective' (2001, p.268). He goes on to say that Hanegraaff's views on the 'Classical' atonement motif are, 'a serious injustice to many orthodox believers' (2001, p.271).

Hanegraaff's typically Lutheran rationalism presumably changed when he joined the Eastern Orthodox church in 2017. Previously, he seemed to imply that unity excludes the reality of various doctrines of the atonement coexisting in orthodoxy together. It is impossible to take Hanegraaff's claims seriously given the lack of historical appreciation. His book 'Christianity in Crisis' is aimed at the 'Word of Faith' movement but in reality, one might suggest that the real 'Crisis' within Christianity has more to do with the divisive mythology that he and the critics have perpetuated in attacking the 'Word of Faith' movement.

Steven Lyn Evans

Orthodox atonement teaching: A brief survey of doctrines

Amongst the various historical doctrines of the atonement Bishop Gustaf Aulén (1879-1978) is well recognized as having successfully differentiated three historical developments. Aulén provides a panoramic view of the atonement throughout Christian history and employs the Ludensian method of motif-research. Others such as Dillistone have offered perspectives that observe many theological doctrines evolving from the wider developments of a culture. In one example out of many in his 1948 book, 'A Christian Understanding of Atonement,' he observes that as British law evolved within society during the Latin period, it impacted theological doctrine to the degree that notions of 'Penal Substitution' evolved. However, for our purposes here, we will concentrate on a general appraisal of the well respected and historically recognized doctrinal theories provided by Aulén.

These will show that the 'Word of Faith' movement has a recognizable referencing of orthodox atonement teachings. It also reveals that the critics have not referenced these doctrines. This lack of recognition of orthodox, historical, theology, by McConnell, Hanegraaff and the critics, serves to confirm the charges that have been made against their efforts.

'Classical' or 'Ransom' theory

The first teaching or 'Classical' type of Atonement emerged according to Aulén with Christianity itself and was popularized by Origen, it remained dominant for a thousand years (1965, pp.49,158). Origen believed that the death of Christ was a ransom that needed to be paid to Satan, who had legal rights over mankind because of 'The Fall.' Aulén regards this view as not being developed in a systematic theological manner, but rather it evolved as more of a motif (1965, p.157). In this view, it is accepted that the death of Jesus was needed to fulfill the agreement that Satan had with God. Without the death of Jesus therefore, lost souls would remain in bondage. Consequently, Jesus became a ransom (Weaver 2001, p.71).

It could be said that the notion of God negotiating with Satan typifies dualistic Greek influences, but this doctrine is complicated further by the idea that in the crucifixion God tricked the devil by hiding the divinity of Jesus under the humanity of Jesus. It has been often noted that this teaching might seem offensive in its acceptance of rights for the devil and the use of trickery, which is deemed inappropriate for God (Weaver 2001, p.71).

Nevertheless, the general Patristic period's teaching was that through this act of representation rather than that of a substitute (Cross & Livingstone 2005, p.124), death is defeated. Aulén has commented that 'Christ having become free among the dead, leads all those who desire to follow Him out of Hades i.e. deaths domain' (1965, p.49). Aulén views the 'Classical' motif favorably and describes Christ within the tradition as 'Christus Victor.' Nevertheless, he concludes that the view has been 'suppressed and met with contempt' because for one thing, it doesn't provide 'fully rational explanations' (1965, p.157).

The critics such as McConnell and Hanegraaff have overlooked the recognizable link between the 'Word of Faith' movement and this 'Classical' motif. In the 1662 Book of Common Prayer from the Anglican Church, we read the following excerpt from the Apostles Creed: 'Suffered under Pontius Pilate, Was crucified, dead, and buried: He descended into hell; The third day he rose again from the dead.' There are several other historical Christian Creeds that highlight Christ's descent into Hell. The Bible teaches us about this: *'For Christ also hath once suffered for sins, the just for the unjust, that he might bring us to God, being put to death in the flesh, but quickened by the Spirit 19 By which also he went and preached unto the spirits in prison; 20 Which sometime were disobedient, when once the longsuffering of God waited in the days of Noah, while the ark was a preparing, wherein few, that is, eight souls were saved by water'* (1 Peter 3:18-20).

However, Hanegraaff has accused the 'Word of Faith' movement of being unaware that the phrase 'descended into hell,' didn't appear in the Creed until the fourth century. He goes on to suggest that, 'it was not part of the original' (1993, p165). Once again, Hanegraaff has shown a poor and inaccurate historical critique. For example, it has been well noted that the 'earliest known mention of the expression 'Apostles' Creed' occurs in a letter of AD 390 from a synod in Milan and may have been associated with the belief, well accepted in the 4th century, that under the inspiration of the Holy Spirit, each of the Twelve Apostles contributed an article to the twelve articles of the creed' (Orr, 1997). So, when Hanegraaff claims the 'descent into hell' wasn't in the original, what original is he referring to? Why does he make this very strong accusation without any subsequent reference? His discovery of an original, different to the one the church has known since the fourth century would be well appreciated. The Christian church would be interested in this most remarkable find! The critics' mythology holds to an audacious methodology.

Hanegraaff calls it 'painful' to quote Tilton on this point, but as we can see, despite Hanegraaff's views on Tilton, what Tilton has written does not go against either the historical Apostles Creed, or the Biblical evidence: 'For three days and three nights he (Jesus) was in the pit of hell, breaking the powers of darkness to set us free' (1993, p163). Kenyon also writes, 'For three days and three nights the Lamb of God was our Substitute in Hell. He was there for us' (1998, p23). DeArteaga recognizes that Kenyon understands the Ransom Theory (2003, p.115). While not all believers might believe this way, we can see that this belief is not peculiar to the 'Word of Faith' movement, this doctrine can be seen within historic Christian theology and this is the key point.

John Calvin taught a similar doctrine according to the Apostle's Creed. He writes, 'Nothing had been done if Christ had only endured corporeal death. In order to interpose between us and God's anger, and satisfy his righteous judgment, it was necessary that he should feel the weight of divine vengeance. Whence also it was necessary that he should engage, as it were, at close quarters with the powers of hell and the horrors of eternal death' (Calvin, II.16.10). The Perriman Report has observed this same point regarding Calvin and suggests that 'Calvin insisted that Christ's bodily death alone would have been ineffectual' (2003, p.269). Calvin and Kenyon might hold the minority position on this point, but history hasn't viewed Calvin's position as heresy and therefore critics clearly ought not to presume to do so with Kenyon and the 'Word of Faith' movement.

As we have seen, Aulén concludes this view has been, 'suppressed and met with contempt' because for one thing, it doesn't provide 'fully rational explanations' (1965, p.157). This contempt can be seen in appraisals by the 'Word of Faith' critics. However, human rationale ought not to be the measure of the Word of God. There has often been a limiting dependency on the ability of mankind to understand with logic, the things of God. For people stuck in this view, the spiritual, the supernatural will be alien. Any notions of miracles will be far off, mountain moving faith will not be employed and faith will be underused.

'Penal Substitution' or 'Satisfaction' doctrine

The second predominant atonement teaching was according to Aulén, the first to be developed into a theological doctrine and was rooted in the West within the Latin period of the Middle Ages (1965, p.143). 'Cur Deus Homo,' was published by Anselm of Canterbury around 1097 A.D. and with it, the predominant understanding of the Atonement shifted from the 'Classical' view to a 'Satisfaction' doctrine.

The new focus was on answering questions about what exactly did the death of Jesus accomplish. Whilst Abelard (1079-1142 A.D.) offered a perspective that focused on Christ's love for mankind and Aquinas (1225-1274 A.D.) went on to develop ideas of the Atonement as being superabundant, it was Anselm (1033-1109 A.D.) who developed the overriding doctrine of a 'Penal substitution' or 'Satisfaction doctrine.' In answering these questions, the death of Christ was no longer understood as a ransom but rather a debt that was owed to God by mankind. Anselm helped introduce the doctrine that the Atonement was payment for the offense that sinful humankind committed against God (Weaver 2001, p.71). He developed a legal 'Penal' methodology, in which Christ Jesus is the 'God-Man' and the honor of God is satisfied through His death (Weaver 2001, p.71; Gorringe 1996, p.122).

'Protestant Orthodoxy' or 'Exchange' doctrine

The third clear teaching of the Atonement was according to Aulén, within the Post Reformation period and is classified under the title 'Protestant Orthodoxy' (1965, p.144). Within this Atonement doctrine there remains a 'Penal' motif but as Aulén suggests, for Luther (1483-1546 A.D.) Anselm's satisfaction theory didn't go far enough. Luther criticizes previous Atonement beliefs, especially those of 'the sophists' who were his theological teachers because they separated Christ from sins and sinners and looked at Christ as merely an example to follow. Luther suggests that the Atonement needs to be viewed as a 'wonderful exchange,' in which Christ is seen as fully exchanging mankind's sins and taking them on Himself. Within this view, Luther rejects the 'Satisfaction' theory and teaches instead that God reckoned with Christ as a sinner, who took the place of mankind. This is often the prevailing view in modern Charismatic movements. However, as has been noted, and will be shown in the next chapter in more detail, the 'Word of Faith' movement has understood all three historical views to varying degrees, often a harmony of these doctrines has been referenced.

Aulén has pointed out that between the 'Classic' and 'Latin' Atonement teachings, there was little 'direct' controversy (1965, p.144). He regards the lack of friction as being the result of a lack of understanding by the Latin exponents who viewed the 'Classical' teaching as a 'hesitating' attempt at expressing their view (1965, p.144). However, there has been tension between 'Protestant Orthodoxy' and the Penal Substitution' view, which has been existent from Luther and especially within the Enlightenment period (1965, p.144).

In conclusion, within this chapter, we have shown that the debate regarding the orthodoxy and roots of the 'Word of Faith' movement has been marred by critical tendencies towards polarization and characterizations. It was established that testing the doctrine of the atonement could provide evidence towards the orthodoxy of the 'Word of Faith' movement. It has also been shown that the Atonement, as a central doctrine of Christianity, provides insight into orthodoxy. Consequently, within the next chapter, it will be possible to show further details of the orthodoxy of Kenyon's and the 'Word of Faith's, atonement doctrine.

Chapter 7

Kenyon's complex fusion of atonement doctrines

Introduction

We will firstly explore Kenyon's fusion of orthodox atonement doctrines, the 'Classical,' 'Penal Substitution,' and 'Exchange' doctrines. It will be shown that Kenyon has, to some degree, adopted all three of these orthodox doctrines. At times, it is difficult to distinguish which doctrine he is referring to, but the vital point is, he is referring to that which is recognizable and historically Christian doctrine.

Thereafter, attention will be given to Kenyon's teaching that Jesus died a spiritual death, popularly referred to by the 'Word of Faith' movement as JDS. The notion of 'Jesus Died Spiritually,' is a part of the wider 'Word of Faith' teaching known as 'Identification.' The JDS teaching has been adopted by the 'Word of Faith' movement's most influential leaders Hagin and Copeland (Perriman 2003, p.73). It has been highlighted by the critics who claimed it was error. As we will see, many significant voices outside of the 'Word of Faith' movement also believe that Jesus died spiritually, in being separated from God.

This chapter is the focal point in the examination of Kenyon and the 'Word of Faith's atonement doctrine. The orthodox atonement definitions within the previous chapter, will provide us with the information to confirm that Kenyon's teaching is recognizably orthodox.

Part A: Kenyon's orthodox combination of doctrines

Firstly, it will be shown that in part Kenyon has taken from all three of the historical Atonement doctrines explored in chapter two by Aulén. According to DeArteaga, these doctrines can be viewed as being complementary to one another, in that they can each be seen as stressing different aspects of the Atonement (1992, p.240). There are orthodox but complicated portions of Kenyon's atonement doctrine which consist firstly, as DeArteaga has noted (1992, pp.240-243), of a 'Classical' ransom motif, often mixed with both the 'Penal Substitution' and 'Exchange' doctrines. The following quotes have been cited because they are consistent with, and typical examples of, Kenyon's complicated harmony of doctrine.

In the first quotation, as DeArteaga has noted (1992, p.241), Kenyon understands Christ's descent into Hades as being part of the 'Classical' ransom motif, however the 'Penal Substitution' doctrine is also present: 'Satan triumphantly bore His (Christ Jesus') Spirit to the Dark Regions of Hades. All the sufferings and torments that Hell could produce were heaped upon Jesus. When He had suffered Hell's agonies for three days and three nights, the Supreme Court of the Universe cried, "Enough." He had paid the penalty and met the claims of Justice. Satan saw Him Justified' (Kenyon 1945, p.89).

Within the above quotation we have a mixture of both the 'Classic' Ransom Atonement motif and later notions of 'Penal Substitution.' Within the words 'Satan triumphantly bore His Spirit' there is a clear reference to the 'Classical' notion that Satan initially considered the death of Jesus as a triumph but was subsequently tricked by God. This 'Classical' teaching as we have previously noted, seems offensive in both its acknowledgment of rights for Satan and the use of trickery, which is deemed as inappropriate for God. However, rather than acknowledging the 'Classical' motif that God tricked Satan, Kenyon links his initial phrase through the 'Supreme Court of the Universe,' to notions of 'Penal Substitution.'

The language of 'He had paid the penalty' describes, as Aulén has noted, the Penal atonement doctrine introduced by Anselm. Anselm put forward the belief that the atonement was payment for the offense that sinful humankind committed against God. Through the death of Christ, the honor of God is satisfied, and atonement takes place. Kenyon's quotation then follows on with the words 'met the claims of justice.' It is not clear however, if Kenyon is referring to Augustinian 'justice,' or the later Protestant penal understanding popularized by Luther.

It is important to consider that the separation between atonement doctrinal theories can be a highly complicated task and not necessarily precise. Kenyon wasn't writing to be theologically precise but rather to convey truth. Whilst the need to distinguish between notions of the 'Classical' ransom representation, and 'Penal' substitution (Cross & Livingstone 2005, p.124) have been made, Morrow has noted that 'the ransom concept has a powerful substitutionary connotation' (1993, p.666). Therefore, within Kenyon's following quotations mention of 'justice' and 'substitution,' there might well be a link to both 'Classical' and later 'Penal' atonement motifs. For Kenyon, it appears that the notion of 'Penal Substitution' is entirely compatible with 'Classical' ransom motifs: 'This revelation from God of the substitutionary sacrifice of Christ, and the fact that He is now seated at the right hand of God having finished a work that perfectly satisfies the demands of justice and meets the needs of humanity' (Kenyon 2004, p.138).

Whilst the language of a 'substitutionary sacrifice' might have strong 'Classical' connotations, it more explicitly suggests a strong Anslem influenced perspective. This influence is further shown by Kenyon's use of the word 'satisfies', which was a keyword for Anslem. Anslem's describes how the honor of God is 'satisfied' through Christ's death, and it is through this sacrifice that atonement is made.

The above Kenyon quotation ends in the words, 'meets the needs of humanity.' This language suggests the doctrine of Luther's 'wonderful exchange,' in which Christ is seen as fully meeting the needs of humanity by exchanging mankind's sins and taking them on Himself. In another quotation, Kenyon further highlights his use of Luther's 'Exchange' doctrine and suggests that: 'There is no ground for salvation through Christ unless he actually took the sinner's place, became sin, voluntarily suffered the extreme penalty of the wrath of God against sin' (McIntyre 1997, p.199).

As Kenyon's initial quotation shows, in combination with the 'Exchange' and 'Penal Substitution' doctrines he regularly punctuates his atonement theology with 'Classical' motifs of victorious ransom language such as: 'He has risen from the conquest of our enemies a Victor' (Kenyon 1998, p.61). This language suggests a similar typology of 'Classical' motifs of Christ rising and leading all who seek to follow Him out of Hades (Aulén 1965, p.157).

Kenyon had merged old and new soteriological notions into his atonement doctrine, this creates at times an unusual, complicated, but not unorthodox fusion. However, he has been criticized for often adopting the unpopular 'Classical' teaching motifs. McConnell for example, is aware of the close connection that Kenyon has adopted with the 'Classical' position (1988, p.123). However, rather than considering the 'Classical' contribution as in any way being orthodox, he suggests that Kenyon and the 'Word of Faith' teachers 'misinterpret' the scriptures (McConnell 1988, p.124). McConnell is categorical in his denial of the 'Classical' atonement doctrine and suggests that 'God doesn't owe Satan a ransom. God owes Satan nothing!' (1988, p.124). In this conclusion, McConnell demonstrates a dismissal of the orthodox historical teaching of the church. His view seems to be all that counts as true, regardless to what has been shown to be the main orthodox, historical position of the church for the first thousand years of its existence (1965, pp.49,158). Indeed, DeArteaga has responded to these arguments and defends the orthodoxy of Kenyon's 'Classical' ransom motif (1992, pp.240-243). McConnell's critique expounds the 'Penal Substitution' claim that, 'the central focus of any doctrine of atonement should be on the fact that Christ's death is a sacrifice to God' (1988, p.123). McConnell seems to believe that this particular view of the atonement is the only view. His dismissal of Kenyon's position is in reality a dismissal of all Christians who have believed similarly for the first 1,000 years of the church especially but also into the present day. It's a very narrow, limited, theological position to hold, McConnell's view seems to be shaped by a desire to create a negative mythology of Kenyon and the 'Word of Faith' movement. Furthermore, for Aulén, perhaps the most influential historical scholar of the atonement, he suggests in direct opposition to McConnell that: 'I believe that the classic idea of the Atonement and of Christianity is coming back' (1965, p.159).

Any assessment of Kenyon's teachings are further complicated by others, even from the side of defending Kenyon's orthodoxy such as McIntyre, who has argued that Kenyon didn't employ a 'Classical' motif at all, but rather the later Anselm influenced, 'Penal Satisfaction' doctrine (1997, p.343). McIntyre has not expounded on his claim by revealing the methodology behind his conclusions. However, the different conclusions reached by defenders of Kenyon, help point towards the claim that Kenyon's atonement doctrine is a complex blend of the 'Classical', 'Penal Substitution' and 'Exchange' doctrines. The real point is that his teaching was orthodox in terms of both a historical and a theological assessment.

The difficulty in classification of the three doctrines has been observed by Morrow in that the substitutionary atonement motif has been generally accepted by theologians in one form or another and can be seen in the 'Classical' ransom motif along with the later Penal doctrines (Morrow 1993, pp.666-667). Furthermore, it is worth considering that the commentaries on Kenyon's theology are often divided in their analysis, in part, because as McIntyre has helpfully suggested, Kenyon was not writing a definitive theology for theologians (1997, p.345).

McConnell and others such as Hanegraaff, have to a considerable degree, based their charges against Kenyon and the 'Word of Faith' movement on Kenyon's supposed links with the metaphysical cults (Hanegraaff 1993, pp.29-30; McConnell 1988, pp.24-26), rather than genuine theological appraisals. Their lack of wider Christian understanding is demonstrated repeatedly. As has been shown, Kenyon also had, in part, a distinctly 'Classical' view of the atonement and it is precisely this view which Aulén suggests the adherents of metaphysics treat with suppression and contempt (1965, p.157). The discovery of this opinion from such a significant figure, offers further weight to the claims of McIntyre and DeArteaga, that Kenyon doctrines were not at all influenced by the metaphysical cults (1997, pp.255-244; 1992, pp.212-223).

Instead, according to DeArteaga, Kenyon ought to be understood as responding to the tide of 'cessationism' and 'the whole realist-materialist assumptions of consensus orthodoxy' (1992, p.212).

Part B: Jesus Died Spiritually JDS

'Jesus Died Spiritually' or JDS is perhaps the most opposed doctrine for the 'Word of Faith' movement and Kenyon's soteriology. It is not surprising therefore that the doctrine of JDS is central to McConnell's critique of Kenyon's atonement teaching. It must be noted that this doctrine isn't overemphasized within the movement, some 'Word of Faith' exponents do not teach this view at all. It is an attempt to theologically understand the extent of the death and subsequent events that led to the resurrection of Christ. As Bowman has noted, the 'Word of Faith' movement's belief that 'Jesus Died Spiritually,' is based on three points:

A) The punishment for our sin is not merely in Jesus Christ's physical death but in His spiritual death also.
B) Jesus Christ died to take our place
C) Therefore, Jesus Christ must have died spiritually. (2001, p.164).

In this analysis, the aim is to show that the notion of Jesus' spiritual death is nothing new to those involved in theological thinking. We will not unpack the various doctrines and implications within Jesus' spiritual death, the aim here is to simply show that authoritative voices outside of the 'Word of Faith' movement also believe that Jesus experienced spiritual death. In this way, we can show that the critics' claims, once again, lack wider referencing and are aimed at creating a metaphysical mythology. The critics have not often cited anyone outside of Kenyon and the 'Word of Faith' movement, holding to the opinion that Jesus experienced a spiritual death. Once again, it seems that the 'Word of Faith' movement's doctrines have been isolated by the critics, this makes them appear entirely separate from the wider Christian church. This lack of balance serves to boost the mythology and fuel the ongoing criticism.

Kenyon first adopted this teaching on reading Isaiah 53:9 where the Hebrew word for death appears in the plural. This was a foundational revelation for Kenyon's JDS atonement doctrine and he suggests that: 'The Hebrew word for death in Isaiah 53:9 is a plural word, showing that Christ's death on the cross was a two-fold death – first a spiritual, and then a physical, as man's substitute' (Kenyon 1998a, p.159). McConnell however, points towards Hebrew scholars such as Keil and Delitzsch who show that the Hebrew language uses the plural for a word when an emphasis of expression is required known as the 'pluralis exaggerativus.' Therefore, he suggests the plural word interpreted by Kenyon from Isaiah 53:9 is merely an emphasis to reveal the harshness of Jesus' physical death. In addition, the Bible repeatedly speaks of Christ dying one 'death' for our sins and not two (John 12:33; Rom. 5:10; 1 Cor. 11:26; Heb. 10:12). However, McIntyre who also cites Keil and Delitzsch, emphases that this plural form of death is only used twice in the entire Old Testament, he goes on to cite the well-respected theologian A.W. Pink, who understood Isaiah 53:9 similarly to Kenyon in that: 'In His (Christ) soul he tasted of the second death, and in His body He suffered natural death; thus He experienced both a physical and a natural Resurrection' (1997, p.341). McIntyre goes on to quote others who also share in the spiritual and physical death theory and the Perriman Report quotes John Calvin on this point: 'Nothing had been done if Christ had only endured corporeal death' (2003, p.110). This is a striking point, by one of the most significant figures in Christian history. John Calvin is confirming the historical validity of Kenyon's view, that on the cross, there was more than a physical death taking place.

As we have seen and will see further, there are significant voices supporting the notion of Jesus' spiritual death, including Calvin, Pink, Pentecost, Gromacki, McIntyre, Lutzer, and Ryrie. This reveals that the critics have once again overlooked wider Christian thought on the subject and their conclusions lack balance. McConnell and the Perriman Report have rightly considered the JDS teaching as being fundamental to 'Word of Faith' exponents. Following on from Kenyon, it has formed part of the core teaching of both Hagin and Copeland (McConnell 1988, p.115; Perriman 2003, pp.22-23). McConnell like Hanegraaff and the subsequent critics has entirely denounced the spiritual death of Jesus, deeming it as 'bizarre' (1988, p.115). Similarly, Hanegraaff has provocatively suggested that the notion of 'JDS' has 'mutilated' the Atonement doctrine (1993, p.162). He concludes categorically that Jesus did not die spiritually (1993, p.177). Perhaps if the critics were aware of the wider theological support towards a spiritual death doctrine, they might have been less emphatic in their denouncing of it. Either way, the critics have failed to engage with the wider theological voices, and this does once again demonstrate evidence towards their intended aim of creating a mythology, as opposed to a genuine theological critique.

Kenyon believed that sickness was spiritual and consequently needed to be addressed in the spiritual realm. Bowman quotes Kenyon regarding this: 'Sin basically is a spiritual thing, so it must be dealt with in the spirit realm' (2001, p.161). It is at this point that the atonement doctrine of Kenyon might seem to have similarities with the metaphysical cults who also maintained that all diseases and subsequent cures were spiritual in origin (McConnell 1988, p.150). On the surface, there might appear to be similarities, however for Kenyon, whilst the antidote to sickness was spiritual, it was not metaphysical and mind centered. This is the vital and fundamental difference. For Kenyon, healing was centered on the redemptive work of Jesus Christ alone. Kenyon wrote, 'It was His (Christ Jesus) Spirit that was declared righteous...It was His Spirit Resurrection that has given to humanity its Redemption' (Kenyon 1998, p.47). Wingate put's it succinctly regarding mankind, 'In receiving the Holy Spirit, they reversed spiritual death' (Wingate pp. 160-161).

In prophecy regarding Jesus' death, Isaiah 53:10–12 reads: *'Yet it pleased the Lord to bruise him; he hath put him to grief: when thou shalt make his soul (Nephesh) an offering for sin, he shall see his seed, he shall prolong his days, and the pleasure of the Lord shall prosper in his hand.11 He shall see of the travail of his soul (Nephesh), and shall be satisfied: by his knowledge shall my righteous servant justify many; for he shall bear their iniquities. 12 Therefore will I divide him a portion with the great, and he shall divide the spoil with the strong; because he hath poured out his soul (Nephesh) unto death: and he was numbered with the transgressors, and he bare the sin of many, and made intercession for the transgressors.'* For exponents of the view that Christ didn't die spiritually, they must interpret the word 'soul' (Nephesh) mentioned repeatedly above, as being limited to the physical body only. The problem with this view is that within the Old Testament, the use of this word 'soul' predominately means the whole of a person, including the physical and spiritual. Therefore, to interpret 'soul' as being limited to Christ's physical body lacks Biblical support. To further illustrate this point, for example, we can consider Genesis 2:7: *'And the Lord God formed man of the dust of the ground, and breathed into his nostrils the breath of life; and man became a living soul (Nephesh)'* [Stegall, 2018]. We can see from this verse that Adam existed in physical form, but it was only when God breathed that he became a living *'soul'* (Nephesh). Before God breathed into him, Adam was just a physical body and a physical body is not described as a *'living soul.'*

One of the key points in understanding Jesus' spiritual death is to define what it means to die. Some have formed their understanding from Genesis by explaining that death in the Bible does not mean that we cease to exist but rather it means a separation. In Genesis, God had warned Adam: *'But of the tree of the knowledge of good and evil, thou shalt not eat of it: for in the day that thou eatest thereof thou shalt surely die'* (Genesis 2:17). The Hebrew, *'in the day'* is clear in its meaning of twenty-four hours. However, Adam continued to live for a total of 930 years on Earth (Genesis 5:5). Obviously, as has been noted by Copeland (2011, p.170), the death warning from God didn't apply to Adam's physical life. Therefore, there is an obvious question, what did the death warning from God to Adam truly mean? We can glean an answer when we consider that Genesis records Adam and Eve hid from the presence of God after they sinned. A separation had taken place, they were by then spiritually dead: *'And they heard the voice of the Lord God walking in the garden in the cool of the day: and Adam and his wife hid themselves from the presence of the Lord God amongst the trees of the garden.9 And the Lord God called unto Adam, and said unto him, Where art thou?'* (Genesis 3:8–10). There was a change in the relationship that Adam had with God. God's warning to Adam was true, Adam died spiritually on the day that he sinned.

Adam's example contributes towards our understanding of how it was possible for Christ to die a spiritual death on the cross. It was a judicial separation from God the Father. In Matthew 27:46 we read: *'And about the ninth hour Jesus cried with a loud voice, saying, Eli, Eli, lama sabachthani? that is to say, My God, my God, why hast thou forsaken me?'* In this verse, Christ is speaking out words from Psalm 22:1 and at that point, sins were judicially imputed to Christ. In 2 Corinthians 5:21 we read more about this event: *'For he hath made him to be sin for us, who knew no sin; that we might be made the righteousness of God in him.'* In Luke's Gospel, it reads: *'And when Jesus had cried with a loud voice, he said, Father, into thy hands I commend my spirit: and having said thus, he gave up the ghost'* (Luke 23:46). In other words, Jesus commended His spirit to God but why did He need to do this? He did this because he was made sin, he had experienced separation from God, in the same way, that Adam did when he sinned. This separation is what is understood as spiritual death.

Prior to Calvary, Jesus' prayed to the Father in Gethsemane, this has a bearing on the question of a physical and spiritual death. In Hebrews 5:7 it reads: *'Who in the days of his flesh, when he had offered up prayers and supplications with strong crying and tears unto him that was able to save him from death and was heard in that he feared.'* In a commentary on this, noted professor of Bible Exposition J. Dwight Pentecost (1915-2014) teaches about Jesus' spiritual death: 'Another explanation is that Christ was praying not concerning physical death, but spiritual death. The penalty for disobedience to God was death (Genesis 2:17). This death was the separation of the sinner from God that is, spiritual death and physical death was the result of prior spiritual death. Therefore, if Jesus Christ was to satisfy the demands of God's holiness, righteousness, and justice to provide salvation for people who are dead, He would have to experience the same death that separated them from God. He must enter into spiritual death, as anticipated in the prophetic 22nd Psalm where the sufferer cried, "My God, My God, why have you forsaken me?" (Psalm 22:1). Here is a mystery deeper than any human mind can comprehend: How could God the Father and God the Son—who are one—be separated one from the other? Yet Christ realized such separation was involved in providing salvation for sinners. Since only that kind of separation or spiritual death could satisfy the demands of a holy, just God, Christ could not have been praying that He would be spared that which was essential' (1992, p.97).

Following on from Pentecost, Robert G. Gromacki, another distinguished professor, also regards Hebrews 5:7 as a direct reference to Christ's spiritual death. He teaches: 'The most plausible position is that He prayed to be delivered from the realm of eternal death, the second death of separation from God. The punishment for sin is both physical and spiritual death (Romans 6:23). At the cross, Christ experienced this double death in order to provide both physical and spiritual redemption for lost humanity' (2002, p.95).

In the New Testament book of Ephesians we read: *'And you hath he quickened, who were dead in trespasses and sins; 2 Wherein in time past ye walked according to the course of this world, according to the prince of the power of the air, the spirit that now worketh in the children of disobedience: 3 Among whom also we all had our conversation in times past in the lusts of our flesh, fulfilling the desires of the flesh and of the mind; and were by nature the children of wrath, even as others'* (Ephesians 2:1-3). In other words, all mankind is classified as being *'dead in our trespasses and sins'* before our salvation. We were nevertheless physically alive, at the point of being classified as dead. Obviously, therefore, the Bible is teaching of a spiritual death, the condition of being separated from God whilst being physically alive.

In conclusion, we have seen in this chapter, it is not only the 'Word of Faith' movement that understands the notion that Jesus Died Spiritually. Many theologians, who are not part of the 'Word of Faith' movement, have clearly written in support of the spiritual death of Jesus Christ. What this clearly does, is establish that the 'Word of Faith' critics such as Hanegraaff McConnell, Peters and those who followed their mythology, have been limited in their appraisals of both general Christian theology and in particular Kenyon and the 'Word of Faith' movement. The methodology of using the orthodox atonement definitions within the previous chapter has allowed for informed conclusions to be reached.

The critics seem to have been unaware that many respected theologians believe that Jesus died spiritually and also that Kenyon's atonement doctrines were a harmony of historical orthodoxy. The irony is, that on closer inspection, their own lack of theological and historical awareness has contributed greatly to their exaggerated and negative appraisals.

Chapter 8

Redemption Realities

The 'Word of Faith' has a supernatural mission

The Enlightenment period developed a significantly less supernaturalistic worldview, which has impacted and often irritated missions towards people that do have a supernaturalistic perspective in life. For example, as Kraft points out when a culture has a supernaturalistic worldview, it views things such as material wealth as signs of the blessings of God (1996, p.189). As we have seen earlier within this work, this was also the Biblical view. However, it is still a highly supported notion within much of the western church that supernatural and material prosperity are not to be interpreted as being connected with the blessings of God (Cotterell 1990, p.12), (Kirk 1999, p.32). Perhaps this fashionable cynicism is born from the echoes of a self-sufficient Enlightenment theology, and delusions of financial self-sufficiency that often exist within the western church.

The 'Word of Faith' movement's leaders have almost all come from modest or poor backgrounds, their emphasis couldn't rest on self-sufficiency as they had too little. Therefore, the movement's emphasis has been on the Bible and what the Bible points towards. There has been a clear emphasis on healing and prosperity as part of the supernatural impact of the Gospel. Scholars such as Kirk, accept that the healing of social evils such as drunkenness, drug addiction, and violence point to the 'life transforming' power of the message preached by healing evangelists (1999, p.220). This impact is transcultural, just as food and water are transcultural, healing and prosperity can also be. Given that the 'Word of Faith' exponents define prosperity as not just the ability to receive, but also having enough resources to give, (Copeland 1992, p.118) the 'Word of Faith' movement is fulfilling this through counteracting poverty.

Western Enlightenment influenced theology, with its Descartes notions of 'Critical Doubt,' might at times be charged with Kraft's claim that, 'western theology seeks to answer questions generated within western societies and ignores those not asked by westerners' (1996, p.88). Along these lines Nussbaum has observed Bosch's omission of the supernatural aspects of mission such as physical healings; he concludes that these omissions might be due to Bosch's 'undetected Enlightenment influences.' He goes on to suggest that as hard as it would be for us to find a German theologian from Bosch's circle of reference who has experienced a miracle; it would be equally hard to find a Chinese or African indigenous church that had not experienced a miracle (2005:151). Nussbaum's point is highly important, and it reinforces Kraft's earlier mentioned points regarding the limitations of western theology. The theology of the critical cessationists such as McConnell, MacArthur and Peters is further exposed by these observations. Further, with a missionary worldview encompassing many cultures, the critics' position is left entirely indefensible.

Sherlock has observed in a definition of wealth, that it is 'the sum total of resources which enrich human living, relationships and service' (1996:106). From this and the earlier mentioned observation of Kraft (1996:189) concerning the blessings of God within material wealth, we might conclude that in having a more supernaturalistic prosperity orientated theology, the church might better facilitate its missionary endeavors. As the Methodist ex-missionary to the poor in Haiti, Philip Potter suggests; 'Christ took on the form or structure proper to God's purpose, so the church must adapt its forms and structures to God's mission today' (Thomas 1995:114). The church has traditionally found it easier to reach out to the poor rather than the wealthy, but as Sherlock observes, 'money matters, and matters considerably in contemporary human societies' (1996:106). Traditional views such as classifying St. Luke as the evangelist to the poor have been challenged, and Bosch cites Schottroff and Stegemann, who have suggested that 'he can more correctly be called the evangelist of the rich' (1991:103). This observation rightly challenges the often well embedded mindsets of western theological rationale.

There can be no doubt that the Christian mission has a legitimate capacity for a gospel of prosperity and health, especially as the church in its missions must relate to a world that is moving fast and often built on modern economic structures. These structures in turn significantly shape nations, and ultimately impact on the world. Critics of the 'Word of

Faith' movement have not appraised the movement's cross-cultural success within these important modern paradigms. Neither have they understood or appreciated the movements ability to have a global impact. In other words, the 'Word of Faith' movement has an ongoing success and has demonstrated a transcultural socioeconomic global ability, to change lives.

Supernatural words of faith

In one of the famous testimonies of Martin Luther we can see that when Myconius a German reformer, wrote to Luther from what he expected was his death bed. Luther's reply sounds like someone from the 'Word of Faith' movement, he wrote: 'I command thee in the name of God to live because I still have need of thee in the work of reforming the church.... The Lord will never let me hear that thou art dead but will permit thee to survive me. For this I am praying, this is my will, and may my will be done, because I seek only to glorify the name of God.' (Myconius, 1911) By the time Luther's letter arrived Myconius had lost his ability to speak but soon enough following the letter's reading, he recovered completely and outlived Luther by two months.

Luther was doing precisely what the 'Word of Faith' movement has taught, he was following the Biblical example of God and *'calling those things which be not as though they were'* (Romans 4:17b). The action of faith is meant to do this, but the critics of the 'Word of Faith' movement have attempted to undermine this Biblical truth. We can see this principle again in the book of Genesis when it records, *'And God said, Let there be light: and there was light'* (Genesis 1:3). We learn from this that God spoke and the light came into being. God spoke out words, and they achieved what they were aimed at achieving. The critics claim, God's spoken word will achieve what it sets out to do, but this power of words does not translate to human beings. However, if we look at the New Testament, we can see various examples that show this power of words does certainly apply to mankind. For evidence of this let's turn to Mark 11: *'And Jesus answering saith unto them, Have faith in God. For verily I say unto you, That whosoever shall say unto this mountain, Be thou removed, and be thou cast into the sea; and shall not doubt in his heart, but shall believe that those things which he saith shall come to pass; he shall have whatsoever he saith. Therefore I say unto you, What things soever ye desire, when ye pray, believe that ye receive them, and ye shall have them'* (Mark 11:22-24). Earlier we saw how important it was to understand Jesus' words, if we are truly followers of

Jesus. Jesus teaches that we are to speak to our mountains, we are to use words with faith, and those words will move mountains.

Let's look at another powerful verse of scripture that testifies to the power of our words. In Romans 10:10 we read, *'For with the heart one believes unto righteousness, and with the mouth confession is made unto salvation.'* It has become popular, but it is an impoverished Bible translation to limit the Greek word salvation here, to the realm of being saved from Hell. The original Greek language makes it clear the word for salvation is transliterated sótéria and according to Strong's Concordance the word means: Salvation, welfare, prosperity, deliverance, preservation, and safety. Therefore, the Biblical mouth confession as taught in Romans 10:10 clearly impacts on many areas of our life. We are to speak out words, and in doing so, those words when accompanied with faith produce positive things in our life including, salvation and prosperity.

The critics will protest and say it doesn't make sense; the Bible believers respond by explaining that the Christian life is a life of faith which is higher than the sense realm. We don't need to understand why or how; we need to believe what the Word of God is teaching us and yield to that. It is by believing that we receive not by understanding (Matthew 21:22). As a Bible teacher, I have attempted to make it easy for people to remember this truth, through the simple and easy to remember catchphrase: Believe and receive or doubt and go without!

Jesus teaches us more on the importance of our words: *'I say unto you, That every idle word that men shall speak, they shall give account thereof in the day of judgment'* (Matthew 12:36). Jesus' teaching is clear, our words ought not to be idle, they ought rather to produce, they are designed to produce. The Greek word for *'idle'* above is 'argos' and it describes words that are idle, lazy, thoughtless and unprofitable. Jesus is warning that this type of speech needs to be avoided and instead, just as Jesus' words produced, just as God's words in Genesis produced everything, mankind's words are meant to produce. In Strongs Concordance regarding the word 'argos,' it highlights the productive aspects of fields, trees, gold, and silver. Therefore, when our words are not idle, we can expect that they will produce good things such as fields, trees, gold, and silver. Again, we see the clear Biblical teaching that our words are meant to generate prosperity for our lives. In the book of Joshua 1:8 it reads: *'This book of the law shall not depart out of thy mouth; but thou shalt meditate therein day and night, that thou mayest observe to do according to all that is written therein: for then thou shalt make thy way prosperous, and then thou shalt have good success.'*

Word of Faith

The English word for 'meditate' means to ponder but in Hebrew, the word is 'Hagah,' meaning to utter, mutter or murmur. In other words, when we meditate on God's Word, we should speak it out, confess His Word, rather than just giving it mental assent. We are to 'Hagah' God's Word by confessing Biblical verses that pertain to the areas that we believe God for breakthroughs in. Many people are waiting for God to make their way prosperous, but the Bible clearly teaches that we will make our way prosperous when we 'Hagah' the Word of God. Our words are undoubtedly vital to our prosperity and success in life. The testimony of Dodi Osteen which will be cited in more detail in this work provides a tremendous testimony in relation to this teaching. She writes, 'I overcame my pity parties by speaking to my body and commanding it to come in line with the Word of God. And it did!' (1986, p.33).

With Dodi Osteen it was a life or death situation, but the power of Words applies to everyday situations. I can remember a simple yet profound example of this that happened to me. It was the day before the official opening of Wales' first Nicklaus Designed Golf Club, named Pentre Nicklaus. The following day there was going to be a big event for the club and area, there was the Professional Golfer and former Ryder Cup Captain Brian Huggett playing an exhibition Golf match, with the course designer Gary Nicklaus. Gary's Father Jack is the worlds most accomplished professional golfer, with a total of 18 major championship wins. The Red Arrows (The Royal Air Force Aerobatic Team) were going to be flying their jets overhead and the first members' competition for the 'Nicklaus Founders Trophy' was taking place. The BBC were also filming the day's events and there was going to be extensive media attention.

Mikah my wife, knew that despite not playing much golf, I would be playing in the 'Nicklaus Founders Day Competition.' She casually told me that she hoped I would win. I then spent a couple of minutes explaining why it was impossible for me to win, I remember saying to her that, "I couldn't win because I hardly play golf these days and most of the players played several times a week." I even said that "It was impossible for me to win!" What was I doing? I was talking myself out of having any expectation of winning the competition with my words. Often people prefer to do this, they set themselves up for failure, rather than victory. This way they can avoid any disappointment taking place. At the end of my negative words, Mikah just said, "I still think you can win." Didn't she hear my explanation? Surely it was impossible, for me to think about winning, but for the next couple of hours, her potent words of belief, kept returning to me, "I still think you can win!"

I reflected more and more on her positive words rather than my negative words. Her words were highly powerful, potent, believing words. Often logic and human reason will oppose such faith and belief, but if you humbly allow these sorts of words into your life, they will cause belief to rise up inside of you. This in turn, will cause you to both reap, and sow, wonderful harvests.

I started to let those words sink into me, they were like seeds sown. I thought, if my darling wife believes that I can win, then at least I can dare to believe with her so that I do my very best. The next step I took, was to consider that, 'all things are possible' and that includes the golf tournament. Those words married with the faith receiver in me, they excited my faith potential, and like all good seeds sown, they started to grow in the soil of my heart. These seeds were growing extremely quickly throughout that day, and so much so, that by late afternoon, I had a transformation in my thinking, and I was saying to myself; "Yes, of course I can win the competition." I was confessing, "With God all things are possible" (Matthew 19:26).

These positive thoughts and confessions continued until the evening time, when my faith had responded so greatly, that I asked Mikah to give me a haircut that evening. I explained to her that I wanted to look smart for the photographs, when receiving the trophy, the next day! Please understand, this wasn't a fleshy boasting statement, I wasn't trying to be funny or even confident, I was simply deeply assured of winning. What was on the inside, was now manifesting out of my mouth, I just saw myself winning the competition.

The ingredients from my part were visualization, faith and confession. The root of this was in Mikah speaking words of faith to me. Think about it, I had gone from having a total lack of expectancy, to total confidence, in just a few hours! Mikah had planted the right words, at the right time, to the right person, and in cooperation with those words, as they were growing inside of me, I spoke them out of my mouth and took the steps required to allow faith into them.

The next day, I won the 'Nicklaus Founders day Trophy.' It was a remarkable thing. Any readers who are club golfers would probably appreciate that shooting a 74 gross on a 74 SSS Championship Golf Course, with a handicap of 9, is very close to impossible. Add to that the fact that I hadn't played golf regularly for many years and the miraculous power of words can be truly appreciated. During the round I remember thanking God for helping me swing the club over every shot and refusing to think negatively. It many ways, it was the most enjoyable round of golf I've ever had. I visualized shots and I remembered reading about Jack Nicklaus as a boy, when he would visualize his shots. In addition, I had believed the Bible could be applied to all areas of my life and confessed what I had visualized. This testimony is due to my darling wife Mikah understanding the wisdom of sowing faith filled words. Remember, *"...all things are possible!"* (Mark 9:23) and *'I can do all things through Christ which strengtheneth me'* (Philippians 4:13).

This is an example of the power of sowing, and receiving positive words of faith, for all aspects of life, whether great or small. Everything you do can be enhanced by understanding and applying a faith mentality. Words will create, so in all things, consider the seeds your sowing, sow positive, good seeds, and reap wonderful harvests, *"...and whatsoever ye do, do it heartily, as to the Lord, and not unto men"* (1 Thessalonians 3:23).

When you receive the words of Jesus, and the soil of your heart is receptive, your life will be transformed, everything you do will be impacted for the better. Soon enough those words will be being spoken out of your mouth. Jesus teaches us that, *'If ye abide in me, and my words abide in you, ye shall ask what ye will, and it shall be done unto you'* (John 15:17).

The critics of the 'Word of Faith' movement simply haven't engaged with the many texts that confirm the potential power of our words. The Bible evidence is clear, we can speak to the mountains and speak prosperity into our lives, words contain the power of God to change our world.

Little gods

The critics of the 'Word of Faith' movement have criticized the teaching that believers are 'Little gods.' Hanegraaff has written, 'Faith teachers take the Scripture's depiction of manmade in the image of God and twist it into a monstrosity' (1993, p.110). He goes on to quote Copeland who teaches 'You don't have a God in you, you are one' (1993, p.110). Hanegraaff's notion of a *'monstrosity'* however, is in truth clear Biblical teaching. Once again, he like the other critics have been shown to be restricted to western anti-supernatural theological traditions.

The Bible position is unequivocal on this teaching, let's look to Jesus words for an explanation first: *'The Jews answered Him, saying, "For a good work we do not stone You, but for blasphemy, and because You, being a Man, make Yourself God." 34 Jesus answered them, "Is it not written in your law, 'I said, "You are gods"'? 35 If He called them gods, to whom the word of God came and the Scripture cannot be broken'* (John 10:33-35). In other words, the Pharisees were the ones who attacked Jesus' teaching about people being 'gods.' Jesus' goes on to say that *'the Scripture cannot be broken.'* In response to this clear teaching, Hanegraaff agrees with the Pharisees and attempts to break the scripture considering Jesus' teaching.

The 'Word of Faith' movement is correct to teach that believers are 'Little gods.' This is in truth, demonstrating humility in submitting to Jesus' teaching, rather than venerating a personal theological opinion. Jesus Himself quoted, *'You are gods,'* if we follow Jesus, we must accept this teaching. Jesus was highlighting the authority that people were given. Jesus' words above are a quote from the Psalms: *'I said, "You are gods, And all of you are children of the Most High"'* (Psalm 82:6). This verse is about the authority to rule with the sanction of God. Barnes' notes on the Bible comment that Jesus 'shows that they ought not to object to his use of the word God, even if he were no more than a man.' (Biblehub.com, 2019). This revelation has proved to be difficult for the religious mind to process. Nevertheless, New Testament believers have been given a greater commission to *'reign in life'* (Romans 5:17) and to represent God as ambassadors (2 Corinthians 5:20). The Bible teaches that, *'I am crucified with Christ: nevertheless I live; yet not I, but Christ liveth in me: and the life which I now live in the flesh I live by the faith of the Son of God, who loved me, and gave himself for me'* (Galatians 2:20).

In teaching this, we can see that Christ lives in us and this again can help us to understand the notion of being 'Little gods.' Believers' words carry authority, we can move mountains, have the creative power of God in our mouths, we confess salvation with our words. A denial of our position as 'Little gods' is in truth, a denial of Jesus' teaching. We have responsibility to live with an awareness of our God-given authority and our representative position in Christ.

The Eastern Orthodox church recognizes a similar emphasis to the 'Little gods' doctrine. They have a doctrine of Theosis, or deification as a transformative process towards union with God. The 'Word of Faith movement's teaching is more practical, and immediate in its description of 'Little gods.' Hanegraaff was forced to acknowledge that theologically the doctrine of 'Little gods' is not heretical (1993, pp.110). However, he then continued to denounce the 'Word of Faith' movement by citing the mythological Kenyon connection to the metaphysical cults. He then went on to firstly accuse the movement of polytheism, and two sentences later claimed they are Henotheistic. It's as if any slur will do for the critics like Hanegraaff, throw enough mud and some is sure to stick! His pathological attack on the 'Word of Faith' movement has allowed for these types of bizarre and absurd claims to be made. The trouble is that to the gullible mind the Henotheistic claim by Hanegraaff might appear to be an interesting revelation. In truth, it is nothing more than an unfounded, inaccurately wild, throw of mud. Henotheism is in truth mostly applied to Hinduism and has nothing remotely to do with the 'Word of Faith' movement.

The Perriman Report concludes its appraisal of this doctrine by suggesting that, 'It must at least be arguable that those who now receive the living Word of God, who are no longer under condemnation, who will live forever, may also be called 'gods' (2003, p.119).

Personal testimonies

As mentioned earlier we have seen many great miracles in our ministry. The ultimate proof for the potency of the 'Word of Faith' positions are the countless miracles that have happened as a result of embracing this Bible-based teaching. For the Enlightenment based western theologians we are entering territory that is hard to understand. For the rest of the world, this is familiar territory based on a clearly Biblical supernatural foundation. Most importantly of all, this is a personal reality which I would not have experienced, had I remained within the confines of western theology. Here are three additional testimonies out of the many hundreds that I could have picked, which demonstrate the reality of the Biblical theology mentioned within this work. It is important to note that these testimonies and the hundreds of others that we have experienced, are the real impetus behind this work. Ultimately, this is not about western notions of theology but rather the Gospel truth, and its substantial impact into our everyday lives.

One day my wife and I had a busy schedule of three long meetings to attend, in the city of Calgary, in Canada. We drove to the first of these meetings, which was due to be the longest, and spent about four hours there.

When we got back into the car on that twenty degrees below freezing day, the lights had been left on, and the battery was now completely flat. My wife Mikah turned the key but there was no power, she tried a couple more times, but the battery was completely flat. I could see she was distraught; tears were flowing, and this would throw us off our tight schedule that day. Immediately, I grabbed Mikah's hand and spoke what my heart believed, and my mind wanted. I spoke to the mountain and said: "Car, I command you to start, now, in the name of Jesus." I believed that it would, and when I told Mikah to turn the key again, sure enough, that car started very powerfully, immediately. The power of spoken words, it was a creative miracle! We kept on the schedule that day and praised God for loving us so much, to have given us the ability to speak words of creative power. When this reality is experienced, one of the greatest benefits is that our relationship and trust in God deepens.

On another occasion, I was driving around the South Wales countryside viewing houses that were for sale, with my parents. Towards the end of the day, we were rushing to view the last house on our list, and I was hoping to find a fuel station to fill the car up. We didn't pass a fuel station so I just continued driving and hoped everything would be alright. Following the viewing, we got back into the car and I turned the key, but the car wouldn't start. My father knew that sound immediately, "It sounds like the car has run out of petrol." I just cringed inside, at my lack of diligence in letting this happen. It was getting dark, and in effect we were now stuck in the middle of the Welsh countryside. My parents were sat in the back of the car, and I apologized to them for letting this happen. Then I told them, that they might not understand what I was going to do next, but I asked them to trust me. Firstly, I prayed to God for forgiveness for not being diligent regarding the petrol. Then I said, "In the authority I have through Jesus Christ my Lord and Savior, I speak petrol into this car, car receive petrol and start in Jesus' name!" Well, I know my parents would think those words were somewhat out of the ordinary, but as soon as I turned the key, the car started! My parents were amazed, my father especially so because he knew the car was completely out of fuel. We drove many miles further through the Welsh countryside before finding a garage. We had just experienced another creative miracle.

Following the front-page newspaper headlines that appeared in Britain because of the many miracles at the church I Pastor, I was invited to speak at a Full Gospel Business meeting one evening. Following the meal, I gave my teaching and testimony regarding the many miracles that we had witnessed. Then the people lined up for the ministry to take place. I waited at the front, and the first person that was brought to me was a woman who was carried by two men. She had a stroke two years previously, and now she couldn't walk or talk clearly, and one side of her body was contorted and frozen. As she was placed in the chair before me, I ministered healing to her in Jesus' name. As I did, the stroke seemed to simply melt off her body, one side was no longer twisted. I then helped her to her feet and slowly she started to walk with hands raised and singing praises to God. The 100 or so people in the room were thrilled by this creative healing happening before their eyes, people were shouting praises to God and they were worshipping God for His healing power, I can recall shouting out, "He's alive!" The key was and always is, refuse to look to the natural evidence and instead look to what the word of God promises. Acting on those promises in faith is what brings results.

I could go on and share testimonies of the lame walking, the blind eyes being opened, the deaf hearing, those with incurable diseases, such as cancer testifying to being completely healed by God. Some of the newspaper headlines are included within this work. Demons have been cast out and the testimonies are tremendous. In many countries, throughout many years, we have ministered healing in Jesus' name. What God does in and through Bible-believing yielded lives, is simply brilliant and way beyond the natural mind. So often this sort of teaching has been ridiculed as being too simplistic, or naive. However, when a person makes a decision to conform their mind to the Bible, rather than conforming the Bible to their mind, the supernatural and the miraculous manifest.

These testimonies are a significant reason for this work. Knowing the 'Word of Faith' movement has helped change so many lives for the better, I was compelled to put the Biblical truth forward. Seeing so many faces filled with joy as people have received their miracles and changed lives, this has been a tremendous privilege for me. God's love compels us towards this Gospel of power and supernatural healing.

Pastoral emphasis

Every movement has its areas of strengths and areas where lessons can be learned. The 'Word of Faith movement' is obviously no different. Strengths in one area can contribute towards a need for development in another. However, strengths can also cause misunderstanding among those who don't share a similar ability or gifting. To this end, Bowman has concluded that at times within the 'Word of Faith' movement, there has been an anti-intellectual aspect (2001, p.223). From the 'Word of Faith' movement's perspective, this position is perhaps a result of observing where the so-called 'intellectual' arm of the church has led people. Often 'intellectualism' has become a codeword for liberalism. These 'intellectuals' have at times, been the first to embrace liberal anti-Biblical trends. The older denominational churches that have embraced so-called 'intellectualism,' seem to be filled with anti-Biblical compromises. The movement, therefore, isn't anti-intellectual, in the dictionary sense of pursuing high ideas but rather, it is anti-liberal. True 'Word of Faith' movement members subscribe for example, to morality of sex within marriage only, and marriage as the union of one man with one woman.

This orthodox Biblical and historical believers' position is often at odds with a so-called 'intellectual' liberal bias.

Many of the leaders within the 'Word of Faith' movement could be rightly classified as highly intellectual in that they have pursued brilliantly creative high ideas and spearheaded world impacting ministries. In any other area of life, this level of excellence would be celebrated as a remarkable achievement.

McConnell has noted there seems to be a lack of counseling for those who are sick and needy (1988, p.164). Along similar lines, the Perriman Report has concluded that there is pressure within the movement to conceal anything that resembles a failure of faith (2003, p.233). Furthermore, McConnell has also suggested that 'faith churches have little or no concept of Pastoral care for the chronically and terminally ill believer.' McConnell goes on to explain that the ill believer is shunned within the movement and regarded with suspicion because believers ought not to be sick, due to the provision for healing within the atonement (1988, p.165).

At times, these apparent weaknesses in the movement are perhaps due in part, to a theological expectation that God's will is healing. There isn't a theology of sickness within the New Testament, but we do find a repeated theology of healing. The 'Word of Faith' movement would obviously always advocate treating those who are ill with love and compassion. If there is a difference of emphasis within the movement, perhaps this has been because a great number of 'Word of Faith' people have testified to experiencing supernatural healing. This will have caused different expectations and would, to some degree, explain the different emphasis.

The testimony of Dodi Osteen is one such example, she was healed of cancer. She was the wife of John Osteen who was a founder member of the International Convention of Faith Ministries (ICFM). She writes the following strong advice for those who are ill: 'Don't sit around and feel sorry for yourself when you are fighting the battle for your healing. Pity never wins! I overcame my pity parties by speaking to my body and commanding it to come in line with the Word of God. And it did!' (1986, p.33). Her tremendously encouraging testimony continues: 'If you are believing God for something, watch what comes out of your mouth. Keep on confessing the Word of God, and God will honor His Word. I want you to believe that there is hope in Jesus. I am a person who has been healed of cancer. I am not anybody special. I am one of God's children just like you are. God wants to help you. He wants you to live. He wants you to live a long, healthy, productive life. But your healing doesn't just automatically happen. You must fight your sickness with God's Word and your faith' (1986, pp.39,40).

Regarding this kind of faith, Bishop Tom Brown quotes from F. B. Meyer's translation of Mark 11:24: *'What things so ever you desire, when you pray, believe that you have taken it'* (Brown 2005, p54). Dodi Osteen did that, she took her healing and has a testimony to the Biblical power provided for believers, to speak to their mountains (Mark 11:23).

This has been the positive emphasis of the 'Word of Faith' movement, their hope has been on healing rather than a less than Biblical and often ineffective 'pastoral concern.' Religion tends to often pamper the senses realm, but belief can change all realms. So often this sort of teaching has been ridiculed as being too simplistic, or naive. However, Jesus calls us to come as children, with belief, and with faith:*'And said, Verily I say unto you, Except ye be converted, and become as little children, ye shall not enter into the kingdom of heaven'* (Matthew 18:3). Dodi Osteen's testimony is a believing example, it reminds us to have faith in the Bible, to resist liberal 'intellectualism' and rather *'become as little children.'*

The love emphasis

In continuation of the pastoral emphasis, it should be noted that the 'Word of Faith' movement, has had a strong emphasis on the importance of love. Copeland teaches that he has chosen to walk in love because: '.... that's what Jesus told us to do' (2011, p.304). This is foundational to Copeland's ministry, and he quotes Jesus' words: *'"But I say to you who hear: Love your enemies, do good to those who hate you, bless those who curse you, and pray for those who spitefully use you"'* (Luke 6:27,28). Hagin also had a strong emphasis on love in his teaching ministry. He and Copeland alike describe the Christian life as the 'Love walk' (2005, p.68) (2011, p.293). Hagin cites the first Christian Martyr Stephen, as an example of someone who showed love to his enemies, he writes, 'He let the love of God dominate him,' to the degree that he, '...prayed for those who were killing him' (2005, p.269). Hagin insightfully explains that in praying for our enemies we avoid being hearers of the Word only, and we become doers of the Word. This ensures that we will be blessed in what we do (James 1:25). Hagin has taught that there are four Biblical responses to our enemies when we pray. We must:

1) Love them
2) Bless them
3) Do good to them
4) Pray for them

He teaches that in doing this, the love of God will be perfected in our lives (2005, p 274). Learning to love, even our enemies, is a great revelation, Jesus words illuminate a very different way to all other ways. If we consider our lives and the walk of faith that we have been called into, that walk can only happen through submitting to the love of God to us, in us, and through us. For faith to work there must be love: *'For in Christ Jesus neither circumcision nor uncircumcision avails anything, but faith working through love'* (Galatians 5:6). I would suggest based on this verse that faith is not working as it was designed to for many Christians because of a lack of love. Love is the vital component. Love is the most essential attribute for the Christian.

In the English language, there is only one word for love, and it has been devalued by overuse. People say for example, that they love a coat, a car, a pair of shoes. Clearly, this is a long way from what the Bible means by the word love. In Greek, there are 4 basic words for love: agápe, éros, philía, and storgē. The strongest word for love is agápe, and it is often found in the Bible. Agápe love is understood by what it does and by what it does not do. It is the love that God has for us, it's unconditional and unending. It is proved by action, agápe love is a verb! We read about this kind of love in 1 Corinthians 13: 4-8a: *'Love (agápe) suffers long and is kind; love does not envy; love does not parade itself, is not puffed up; 5 does not behave rudely, does not seek its own, is not provoked, thinks no evil; 6 does not rejoice in iniquity, but rejoices in the truth; 7 bears all things, believes all things, hopes all things, endures all things. 8 Love never fails.'*

Agápe love is not based on feelings or circumstances it is of a more profound commitment. This love keeps on loving even when the loved one is unresponsive, unkind, unlovable, and unworthy. It is an unconditional love that desires only the good of the one who is being loved, it is a consuming passion for the well-being of others. Christians must, according to Jesus Christ, have agápe love for one another. Jesus said: *'A new commandment I give unto you, That ye love one another; as I have loved you, that ye also love one another. 35 By this shall all men know that ye are my disciples, if ye have love one to another'* (John 13:34,35).

Chapter 9
Further issues for the critics

Contextualization

Critics of the 'Word of Faith' movement such as the mythology makers McConnell, Hanegraaff, MacArthur and Peters are devoid of explanations regarding the success of the movement in terms of its global impact and its contextualization. The critics have failed to grapple to understand the intrinsic methodology of the movement, which the movement attributes to its biblical emphasis. The critics, who have created a mythology of linking the movement with metaphysical cults, have in doing so, alienated themselves from the true Pentecostal and Charismatic roots of the movement. This in turn, has led to an inability to understand the movement accurately and appreciate its ability to contextualize the 'Missio Dei' successfully. In using 'Missio Dei' I'm referring to the theological term translated as 'Mission of God' and meaning God's work through the church.

Gilliland has given a definition of contextualization as a tool: 'to enable, insofar as it is humanly possible, an understanding of what it means that Jesus Christ, the Word, is authentically experienced in each and every human situation' (Gilliland, 2000). It has further been observed by Hiebert, that there are four different levels of contextualization:

1) No contextualization: Christian faith is understood as not being part of human culture, this view lacks the reality of practical experience.
2) Minimal contextualization: A recognition that differences exist between cultures, but they limit cultural influences into the gospel.

3) Uncritical contextualization: A liberal construct emphasizing culture over the Gospel in which Biblical truth is submitted to culture.
4) Critical contextualization: The Bible is seen as divine revelation that cannot be compromised, cultural awareness is employed, but it is not valued higher than Biblical truth (2010, pp.84-99).

The processes of the 'Word of Faith' movement have instinctively recognized aspects of contextualization. They have then been able to take culture and present unchanging Biblical truth through them. Within the unique and changing contexts of cultures and worldviews, the 'Word of Faith' movement, has been remarkably successful in its contextualization. It has managed to communicate Biblical truth into a global network of believers. This lends significant evidence towards the transforming cross-cultural ability of Biblical truth to penetrate supernaturally into people's lives. This view is, in the main, foreign to western theology but the Bible teaches: *'For the word of God is quick, and powerful, and sharper than any two-edged sword, piercing even to the dividing asunder of soul and spirit, and of the joints and marrow, and is a discerner of the thoughts and intents of the heart'* (Hebrews 4:12).

We can see that the 'Word of Faith' movement has used scriptural principles as their foundation for mission and that there is significant evidence testifying to the success of this emphasis. For an example of how the movement has been able to reach out into differing cultures, we could look at 'Word of Faith' minister, David O. Oyedepo who is the Nigerian Christian founder and presiding bishop of the megachurch Faith Tabernacle, a 50,000 seat church located in the area of Canaanland which the church established. This has been reported to be the largest church auditorium in the world according to the Guinness World Records. Oyedepo oversees the international network of Living Faith Church Worldwide which is also known as Winners' Chapel. This international church network is in over 300 cities and has a remarkably successful impact in spreading the Gospel with an emphasis on prayer, Bible study, devotion to God, faith, success and victory through Jesus Christ. Oyedepo is an extraordinary pioneer and was named in 2011 by Forbes magazine as being the richest pastor in Nigeria (Mfonobong, 2011). Copeland attended the 36th anniversary service of Faith Tabernacle in Nigeria as the guest speaker, and he has had an ongoing and close connection with his 'Word of Faith' colleague. Clearly, the 'Word of Faith' message has resonated successfully with millions of people in Africa and around the world. Through Oyedepo's Living Faith

Church network alone, they have churches in 45 African nations, hundreds of schools, several universities, hospitals and have transformed significant portions of African society.

Reasons for the 'Word of Faith' movement's missionary success

1) An authentic belief in the Biblical truth often underestimated in modern western theology.
2) There is an emphasis on personal integrity and holiness.
3) An easily translatable message of victory in life through Christ.
4) An absolute message that includes healing and prosperity.
5) An easily repeatable model for growth.
6) A lack of religious hierarchy and obstructing structures.
7) Many opportunities to excel in personal gifting.
8) There is little to hinder the path to leadership.

The main developments within the mission strategy of contextualization offer support for the adoption of a greater openness towards so-called 'Third World' and non-western theological positions. We have seen this above in the case of Oyedepo and as previously mentioned within this work, in the commitment shown by the Mozambique government to the teaching of Copeland and his 1974 book, 'The Laws of Prosperity.'

The critics of the 'Word of Faith' movement have failed to contextually understand the movement. As we have seen, the 'Word of Faith' movement gained momentum in the latter half of the twentieth century. This is an important point that has been lost to the critics whose mythology looks further back to Kenyon. The twentieth century saw a significant development of day to day luxury in the average western home. For the first time many families were enjoying the development of cars, fridges, indoor plumbing and lighting, cookers, airplanes, transport networks of various kinds etc. The prosperity of many western countries gained great momentum after the Second World War. Consequently, the average family at the end of the century lived in comparative luxury to a family at the start of the century. Not even Kings and Queens at the start of the century could have imagined that life could have contained so many different types of luxuries so close at hand.

As a consequence, to these developments, we need to recognize that the days of the village Parson on a bicycle were largely over. The world had become a village and the days of ministry via the internet, satellite television and jet aircraft had arrived. The critics have entirely overlooked sociological contextualization and its ability to interpret trends in society. Given the significant sociological developments within society, the use of ministry jets and the success of ministers with lifestyles that look lavish become easier to understand. Or to put it another way, football players, company directors and salespeople travel on private jets. There is therefore no reason why a minister within that culture, should not have a similar level of transportation available to them.

It is important to remember that contextualization is often limited itself, by its own particular bias from within its own limited context. In western theology this perspective is born out of a Higher Criticism methodology and generally has adopted an anti-supernatural bias in its reading of biblical texts. The 'Word of Faith' movement on the other hand, is clear that the only way to understand the biblical texts is with a supernatural perspective.

This coupled with the optimism of the movement delivers hope and expectancy, which are thoroughly appropriate to the gospel of the Kingdom of God. The Perriman Report observes that 'If Word of Faith teaching overstates the dynamic of fulness and abundance and victory in the Christian life, this is largely as a corrective to the apathy and negativism that dominates the Christian mindset in the West' (2003, p.219).

The authenticity of a supernatural emphasis

An important observation has been made by scholars such as Nussbaum who observes that for most people within an African, Latin American or Chinese context to demythologize the miracles in the Bible would be equally as unbelievable as the miracles appear to systematic theologians (Nussbaum 2005:151). It seems that from the popularly liberal western theological perspective, demythologizing is essential for intellectual congruence but equally essential from the 'Third World' non-western perspective is congruence in the Bible and the miracles testified to within it. There exists a seemingly diametrically opposed framework of beliefs between these perspectives. It is interesting to note that recent trends have seen western scholars begin to take seriously, the theological positions found within 'Third World' non-western contexts. Charles Kraft has criticized much of western intellectualized doctrine and suggests that mission practice requires more Spirit-power based behavior (1996:211).

Kraft is not alone in his perspective, and Bosch considers Kraft's work in the field of inculturation, which is cynical towards western theological systems, to be of such significance that it is 'pioneering' (1991:452).

According to Kraft systems of western theological analysis are mainly bound to exclusively Western methodologies and are entirely different to the methods employed by the majority of the rest of the world (1996:88). These methodologies can be traced back to the Enlightenment, and Kraft even suggests that Theology can be seen as being entirely western, he goes on to suggest that western theology is 'largely captive to western cultural ways of thinking' (1996:88). This helps to explain why the 'Word of Faith' movement has been attacked so vigorously, the theological paradigms used to assess the movement have been limited by both the prevailing anti-supernatural cessationist perspective and the mythological Kenyon connection.

We can clearly trace the roots of western systematic theological approaches back to the Enlightenment period. Bosch makes an insightful observation and suggests that the problem with the Enlightenment influenced approach is that western theologians 'did not realize that their own interpretations were as parochial and as conditioned by their context as those they were criticizing' (Bosch 1991:423). Concerning the 'Word of Faith' critics, they have betrayed their cessationist anti-supernatural bias. This bias is so penetrating that, as we have shown within this work, it has impacted their ability to offer either theological or historical accuracy.

It could be said that paradoxically, the Enlightenment-based theological systems, were blinded by the very light that they claimed was illuminating their way. This observation is taken even further by Nussbaum who suggests that the Enlightenment theologians, 'were trying to remove the cultural splinter from the eye of the biblical writers without considering the cultural plank in their own eyes' (Nussbaum 2005:108). Nussbaum reveals a growing awareness within theological development that is no longer prepared to defend the presumed theological supremacy of western theological systems of analysis, over any others.

Western theology has often been unable to provide satisfactory answers to the many varying contexts of emerging marginalized voices, and Nussbaum has suggested: 'theology that is a bystander in the battle of the oppressed and oppressors cannot be true to God' (Nussbaum 2005:108). Again, this is where we can see the strength of the 'Word of Faith' movement. It has offered supernatural and practical theology into the most impoverished global situations, providing a great hope and also subsequently, countless positive personal testimonies.

It has been observed by Nussbaum, that in opposition to the 'Word of Faith' perspective, western theologians generally 'think and write as if knowing, understanding and explaining are the only valid aims of theology' (Nussbaum 2005:108). Critics of the 'Word of Faith' movement often come from this viewpoint and have been restricted in understanding within its limitations. The 'Word of Faith' movement could be seen as having adopted a transcultural 'Biblical context.' Historically since the nineteenth century, older western missionary thinking had adopted a position that their emphasis was 'supracultural and universally valid' (Nussbaum 2005:107). Often, for example, absolutes such as the need for food, healing, water, goods, and medicine, can be translated in a supracultural way. The 'Word of Faith' movement is not only transcultural but has proved that when the mission has a Biblical emphasis, it can be supra-cultural and therefore to varying degrees, universally valid. In claiming to be supracultural we are recognizing that Biblical functions and directives can be applied to all cultures of the world and at any time in history, with potentially equal potency. This is not taking away the need for context and appropriate application According to Christian anthropologist Charles Kraft, systems of western theological analysis are bound to exclusively Western methodologies and are entirely different to the methods employed by the majority of the rest of the world (1996:88). These methodologies can be traced back to the Enlightenment, and Kraft suggests that Theology can be seen as being entirely western. Kraft goes on to suggest that western theology is 'largely captive to western cultural ways of thinking' (1996:88). He further suggests emphatically that 'mission practice requires more Spirit-power based behavior' (1996:211).

The critical cessationists

Firstly, let's consider what does it mean to truly be a follower of Jesus? Well, to answer that question let's consider how we would describe someone who was not following Jesus? Some antonyms for the word follow are, disregard, misunderstand and neglect. To truly follow Jesus therefore, we must have regard, understanding, and pay attention to His teachings toward us.

For the critics of the 'Word of Faith' movement, it is impossible to maintain the theological integrity and reduce Jesus' clear New Testament teaching in the ways they have. Many of the critics of the 'Word of Faith' movement such as McConnell, MacArthur, Hunt and Justin Peters for example, are cessationists. Cessationism advocates for the clearly un-Biblical position which claims that spiritual gifts such as speaking in tongues, prophecy, casting out of demons, healing, and other supernatural activity, ceased with the apostolic age. They seek to reduce and in effect discredit Jesus' words and the entire New Testament to their restrictive doctrine. From this anti-Biblical standpoint, they then have the temerity to present themselves as a sort of spiritual police-force examining the Christian world for heresy. They can see faults everywhere, but the glaringly obvious errors of their own heresy have been well overlooked.

Jesus taught for example, *'And these signs shall follow them that believe; In my name shall they cast out devils; they shall speak with new tongues; 18 They shall take up serpents; and if they drink any deadly thing, it shall not hurt them; they shall lay hands on the sick, and they shall recover'* (Mark 16:17, 18). So according to Jesus Christ, who the critics confess to be following, there are *'signs that will follow them that believe.'* Let's look at these signs in part here and examine if they are in evidence within the 'Word of Faith' movement? Also, let's ask if they are evident in the critics of the 'Word of Faith' movement? The signs Jesus taught about are:

1) Cast out devils.
2) Speak in new tongues.
3) Lay hands on the sick and they shall recover.

All three of the above are evident in the 'Word of Faith' movement. Further, all three of the above are not evident in most of the critics of the 'Word of Faith' movement such as MacArthur and Peters. Further, they emphatically disapprove of those who do follow Jesus' ministry work. We must conclude from this simple observation that the critics are not following Jesus' teaching. Their views must, therefore, be rejected by followers of Jesus' teaching. Also, the critics need to fundamentally address the issue of where the authority for their cessationist ideals is found, given the utter lack of Biblical support for this position.

Jesus teaching in Mark 16 above and many other passages of the New Testament are merely relegated to history for the cessationists. There is not one verse within the New Testament teaching that suggests spiritual gifts or supernatural ministry was to end with the Apostolic age. As we will soon see, John Wesley the eighteenth-century leader of the Methodists, soundly denounced the cessationist position for its anti-Biblical stance. In this observation, we find the strange irony of the critics. The critics have often been known as the 'Heresy hunters.' The Webster dictionary defines 'Heresy' as 'An opinion, doctrine, or practice contrary to the truth or to generally accepted beliefs or standards.' Therefore, the 'Heresy hunters' are in truth the ones who have embraced heresy. They have attempted to disguise their heresy by portraying themselves as those who are scrutinizing other ministries for heresy.

Justin Peters promotes the mythology invented by McConnell. On his website, Peters advertises the seminars he promotes as being, 'a fair, comprehensive, biblical critique of the modern Word of Faith movement' [Peters, 2018]. However, Peters is another in a line of critics who promote the mythology that the movement originates in the late 19th century with Quimby's metaphysics and Mary Baker Eddy's Christian Science. As we have established the theological and historical evidence does not support this view. In addition, the leading academic research on the 'Word of Faith' movement fundamentally disagrees with this theory. Any claims to be 'fair' therefore, are exposed and found wanting by the theological and historical evidence. In truth, if the critics want to demonstrate fairness, they will first need to recant the mythology and accept that the 'Word of Faith' movement is not cultic.

The importance of having a Biblical based ministry and following Jesus' words ought to be self-evident. It is highlighted when we consider that Jesus' words are not mere theological theory but rather, vital life impacting truth. We can see this for example, in the case of the Cambridge scholar and noted Bible teacher Derek Prince. Prince's teachings were very much in line with the 'Word of Faith' movement, but as a young minister, he wrestled for years with depression. He prayed, fasted, studied the Bible, made resolutions but still, there was no breakthrough, things seemed to get worse.

Prince testifies that a life-changing revelation came to him from Isaiah 61:3. *'To console those who mourn in Zion, To give them beauty for ashes, The oil of joy for mourning, The garment of praise for the spirit of heaviness; That they may be called trees of righteousness, The planting of the Lord, that He may be glorified.'*

Prince says that when he read the phrase the *'spirit of heaviness,'* by revelation, he suddenly saw that his problem was a person. He teaches, 'Even though it was an invisible spirit without a body, it was still a very real person. A spirit of heaviness, or depression, was systematically attacking me. The powerful oppressor who had been seeking to destroy me and to ruin my ministry had been exposed. That evil was not something; it was someone—and the time had come for me to overcome him. With this realization, I was 80 percent of the way to victory. Then I remembered that this was a family problem. My father, and probably his father, had fought this very same battle for years. To gain complete victory over that awful spirit of depression, I needed only one other Scripture: "It shall come to pass, that whosoever shall call on the name of the Lord shall be delivered" (Joel 2:32). When I called on the Lord specifically to be delivered from the spirit of heaviness, in the name of the Lord Jesus Christ, quoting Joel 2:32, I was delivered!' (2017, pp.13,14). Prince went on to have a ministry that impacted millions of lives, and this powerful testimony is a reminder that Jesus' words about *'cast out devils'* (Mark 16:17) are not mere theory but a practical truth that must be applied.

The cessationist position is without Biblical justification and is clearly anti-Biblical. Jesus said, *'Most assuredly, I say to you, he who believes in Me, the works that I do he will also do; and greater works than these he will do because I go to My Father'* (John 14:12). The cessationists deny that Jesus' words apply today. Furthermore, they then pursue faithful believers and denounce people who do believe in Jesus' words! The Biblical warning in 2 Timothy 3 teaches about perilous times in the last days and about *'slanderers'* in verse 3 and people who *'Having a form of godliness but denying its power. And from such people turn away!'* (2 Timothy 3:5). In other words, if there's no supernatural power, no miraculous works they are not of God. The form of Godliness is the mere theory, the outward show, but lacking in the authenticating miraculous power of God.

These miracles and the casting out of demons serve to highlight the errors of the cessationist critics such as MacArthur and Peters. They push an outwardly respectable Gospel on some levels, but it denies Jesus' commission to the church, denies the Bible, denies church history, and denounces those who disagree. The theology rejects the miraculous and reduces Jesus' words to historical text. In this way, they usurp the Bible, they hold to their authority as being above scripture and from that vantage point, it's little wonder that they maintain such a critical perspective towards people who follow the Bible.

The critics' denial of the Bible is obvious and shown repeatedly. They then take their errors further by attacking those who have taken Jesus' commission seriously and are engaging in the supernatural realm. Jesus' clearly teaches us that there is power for believers when the *'...Holy Spirit has come upon you'* (Acts 1:8). This power to witness must be in accordance with Jesus' teaching regarding the signs of those who believe and include demonic deliverance, healing and new tongues (Mark 16:17,18). Their position is not merely wrong, but it is grossly anti-Biblical denying the truth about Jesus' commission to His church.

Other critics don't claim to be cessationists but nevertheless show skepticism towards supernatural events within their positions. These critics do not truly engage with the 'Word of Faith' movement's beliefs, rather they have created a caricature of the movement's beliefs and use the mythological link to the metaphysical cults in an attempt to dismiss them.

One of the further other issues for the critics is that the 'Word of Faith' movement is open to love and encourage other Christians, despite differences in theology. The critics, on the other hand, are intolerant of differing positions. Anyone who doesn't believe in MacArthur's narrow Bible-denying cessationism is regarded as apostate. MacArthur saw fit, for example, to even attack the noted and well-respected evangelist Billy Graham accusing him of apostasy.

Bowman's classifications

Every movement has its areas of strengths and areas where lessons can be learned. The 'Word of Faith movement' is no different. Strengths in one area can contribute towards a need for development in another. In addition, strengths can also cause misunderstanding among those who don't share a similar ability or gifting. To this end, Bowman has concluded that at times within the 'Word of Faith' movement, there has been an anti-intellectual aspect (2001, p.223). From the 'Word of Faith' movement's perspective, this position is perhaps a result of observing where the so-called 'intellectual' arm of the church has led. These 'intellectuals,' have often been the first to embrace liberal anti-Biblical trends. The older denominational churches that have embraced so-called western 'intellectualism,' seem to be filled with anti-Biblical positions. The movement, therefore, isn't anti-intellectual, but rather anti-liberal.

In 1992 when Bowman was assessing the 'Word of Faith' movement for the Christian Research Institute, he recognized that different Christian groups often have a complicated blend of orthodox and unorthodox teachings. The Christian Research Institute at the time was led by Hanegraaff and so it would have been difficult to expect, given Hanegraaff's criticism of the movement, that a fair and balanced appraisal could be found. Nevertheless, Bowman's conclusions were essentially different from Hanegraaff. He chose to reject the notion presented by popular critics such as McConnell and Hanegraaff that the 'Word of Faith' movement is cultic (2001, p.228). The Perriman Report agrees with Bowman and suggests regarding dialogue with the 'Word of Faith' movement that, 'One approach would be to accept that the core Word of Faith doctrine is sound' (2003, p.210). It offered a further positive view of the 'Word of Faith' movement in their suggestion that 'there is a large enough overlap between the Mainstream church and 'Word of Faith' movement to justify a serious commitment to work together to understand and resolve the causes of division' (2003, p.230). The causes of the division have come from the critics and their divisive mythology of the movement.

Some 'Word of Faith' teaching, as has been observed by Bowman, can be traced back through Copeland, to Hagin, and eventually to the doctrines of Kenyon. Bowman created a table of reference for the purposes of detailing his classifications. This systematic appraisal has been done in response to the charges of 'cultic' that have been made by McConnell and those who followed him. Within the table, Bowman has cited 23 of the most important topics to the New Thought Metaphysical cults. Bowman has then created two further columns one of which represents the emphasis of the Christian Science movement, and the other which details Kenyon's emphasis.

Whilst the Christian Science movement shared an emphasis with the metaphysical cults in 16 of the 23 subject categories, Kenyon only shared an emphasis in 6 of them (2001, p.47). Even this small similarity of emphasis is debatable, in that there might be a technical subject connection but not a deeper doctrinal connection. Nevertheless, the significant differences of doctrine revealed by this table have led to Bowman's suggestion that McConnell's critique of Kenyon is not supported by a critique of Kenyon's words but rather McConnell attempts to fill in the significant gaps by quoting from Hagin and Copeland (Bowman 2001, p.48).

In Bowman's conclusion, he suggests that: 'Kenyon differed radically from all of the metaphysical cults on a number of essential theological and philosophical matters. Thus, we cannot classify his teaching as belonging in the metaphysical tradition' (2001, p.47). From a work colleague of Hanegraaff, this conclusion is striking.

Chapter 10

Issues For the 'Word of Faith' movement

Introduction

This book was born out of my own personal journey as a follower of Jesus Christ. It is not the mere theory of some distant theology; it is based on the reality of my life which was transformed through encountering the 'Word of Faith' movement. I had grown tired of the pretensions and cynicism of much within modern theological enquiry. Within the 'Word of Faith' movement, there was a devotion to the Word of God as authoritative, it provided a mandate for Christian life and victory. I was hearing about a living faith, victory in Jesus and the abundant life that He promised (John 10:10).

Nevertheless, the 'Word of Faith' movement, like all movements, has areas that could be strengthened. There are areas where confusion and errors have been prone to develop. Within this work, it has been shown that the 'Word of Faith' movement has substance behind its history and theology. This is not to say that the 'Word of Faith' movement doesn't have the need for circumspect assessment, it does. There has been a danger for some to take things to extremes, for teachings to be pushed beyond Biblical truth. Teachings at times, have been both misunderstood and misapplied.

The movement has developed a culture of faith and believing. Often this has been a tremendous blessing but there have been times when some have not appropriated enough meaning and walked in presumption. This is what Charles Farah was exploring in his book, 'From the Pinnacle of the Temple,' when he was McConnell's Theological Professor at Oral Roberts University. Take for example, the scripture that teaches that we can *'Believe and receive'* (Matthew 21:22). I recall the well-known testimony of Kenneth Copeland, who when teaching at a Bible College, told the students how God had once called him to 'sow' his car into a ministry. A short time later, he received a new car in return. Several of the students, listening enthusiastically to Copeland that day, took his personal testimony and ran with it for themselves. They gave away their cars and then waited for their new ones to arrive. When the new cars didn't arrive, they were forced to do a lot of walking that year! What went wrong? They were not meant to 'sow' their cars, they had taken someone else's 'Rhema' (The spoken and particular word of God) and in effect, tried to turn it into 'Logos' (The written and general word of God). We can't take what God has called someone else to do and presume that it will work for us. As Hagin observed, 'God's specific, personal direction for one individual does not become an across-the-board doctrine for the whole Church. There is no spiritual formula to sow a Ford and reap a Mercedes' (2000, p.119).

The 'Word of Faith' movement has been strong in offering absolutes in the realms of Biblical teaching, but these can become presumptions for some, if they lack wisdom. The written Word (Logos) is our foundation and God quickens a verse to a believer through the Holy Spirit for a specific time and purpose. The immature students who gave their cars away, had mixed 'Rhema' and 'Logos' up. For some, the disappointment of not receiving what they expected, might lead to questioning the teaching of *'Believe and receive.'* However, the teaching isn't the problem, it's the understanding and application of the teaching that is the issue. Sadly, there have been many examples of people not employing wisdom. There is a Godly order and it includes wisdom, truth, timing, and God's will. Ephesians 5:17 puts it this way: *'Wherefore be ye not unwise, but understanding what the will of the Lord is.'* Hagin has observed that 'even sincere, honest people can allow their zeal for truth to exceed their wisdom' (2000, p.153). Knowing the will of God with wisdom is vital, presumption through a lack of wisdom, can lead to disappointment and imbalance.

Previously within this work we have looked at theological and historical issues. We have shown through detailed analysis that the 'Word of Faith' movement has often been unfairly attacked and a critical mythology has been created. Here, we will touch on further issues that the movement has had to deal with, which the critics have often sought to use in support of their attacks.

Balanced prosperity

The critics have been aided at times, by some ministries, who have had unhealthy biases. These have contributed negatively towards the 'Word of Faith' movement, for example, whenever a television minister asks viewers for money, people often wrongly presume that they belong to the movement. Some people for example, might use sowing and reaping scriptures, it might sound a little like the 'Word of Faith' message but it often ought to be distinguished from authentic 'Word of Faith' teaching. In saying authentic, we're looking to the teachings of Hagin and Copeland who are the recognized historic leaders of the movement.

Hagin and Copeland are not the ones who beg, plead, and involve practices which could be deemed to be manipulative, regarding money on television. Their emphasis, as has been shown, is diametrically opposed to this. Hagin comments regarding such things for example: 'Some gimmicks are absolutely ridiculous, and the fact that they seem to work just illustrates how unlearned and superstitious many people are. They are prisoners of the soulish realm and do not live in the spiritual realm. Years ago, someone on the radio talked about a red string he would send you for an offering of $10. It was supposed to have special power in it. If you were fat, wearing the string around your waist would cause you to lose weight. If you were skinny, wearing the red string would help you gain weight. Then someone came up with the idea of blessed billfolds that had been prayed over. People could get them by sending the minister a $25 offering. People were supposed to put the billfold in their pocket and expect God to miraculously fill it up with money. After carrying it a while, people were supposed to open the blessed billfold and find that money had been supplied to pay their bills. I know it seems impossible that anyone would be deceived by something so silly, but many sent in their money and used those red strings and blessed billfolds. Other gimmicks may seem more believable and convincing' (200, pp.142-143). Clearly, the 'Father' of the 'Word of Faith' movement, distanced himself entirely, from the spurious tactics that are often seen on television.

The movement has, through the example of Hagin and Copeland, held to a sincerity of belief in the supernatural funding of ministries. Copeland and Hagin alike, have advocated financial provision through Biblical faith principles. In 1950 Hagin had the following revelation, 'The Lord said to me, "Don't pray about money like you have been. Whatever you need, claim it in Jesus' Name. And then you say, 'Satan, take your hands off my money.' And then say, 'Go, ministering spirits (*Angels*), and cause the money to come'" (2000, p.35). Hagin testifies to the results of this revelation, 'With no emphasis or pressure, the amount of my offerings began to increase, and the needs of my family and my ministry were met' (2000, p.37).

Enlightenment influenced western theology doesn't have the appropriate tools of interpretation for this type of emphasis. This emphasis involves revelation knowledge which is birthed from a supernatural perspective. This spiritual emphasis has helped the 'Word of Faith' movement avoid many of the bizarre tactics of some of the televangelists. It is worth noting that the critics classifications of ministries are often unable to distinguish true 'Word of Faith' ministries from others.

As previously noted, Copeland has criticized greed and the western desire to use prosperity as a means of selfish comfort especially the 'provision of more conveniences and luxuries' (1985, p.46). He admits that he had been 'guilty' at one time of pursuing the comforts of wealth, but subsequently, he 'repented' (1985, p.46). Whilst believing in financial prosperity is entirely appropriate for believers, there is a danger in people overemphasizing and focusing too much on finance. The many Biblical warnings regarding finances ought not to be overlooked. Hagin warns that 'The lie of covetousness is: "If only I had more money," or "If only I had such and such, I would be happy." But contentment says, "Because of Jesus Christ, I am happy no matter what the circumstances"' (2000, p.186).

Nevertheless, the 'Word of Faith' movement has had people who have missed the mark in the area of prosperity. Hagan was aware of these issues regarding finances within the movement and his book 'The Midas Touch,' was aimed at encouraging people to pursue Biblical balance. Hagan writes, 'There are those in the ditch on one side of the road who teach that Jesus lived in abject poverty, that money is evil, and that biblical prosperity has nothing at all to do with material things. And in the other ditch, there are people who are preaching that getting rich is the main focus of faith, that God's main concern is your material wellbeing, and that money is the true measure of spirituality. Where is the truth? It's found far away from both extremes, on much higher ground' (2000, p.XIV).

The higher ground that Hagan was advocating involved Biblical balance he explains: 'It grieves my spirit to hear that there are some ministers teaching, or at least giving the impression, that giving to them personally will bring a greater blessing to the donor than giving to the poor or supporting the local church's ministry to the poor. Again, these individuals imply that because they have a "special anointing" like Jesus, they have a gift, a Midas touch, to multiply money back to the donor and impart great blessings. Some of these ministers actually suggest that there is not much blessing in giving to the poor by quoting Proverbs 19:17: *"He that hath pity upon the poor lendeth unto the Lord; and that which he hath given will he pay him again."* "That's not too good an investment," they say. "Giving five dollars to a poor person is a loan to God, and He will pay you back five dollars. You get back just what you 'loaned' to God. But if you invest that five dollars in a ministry with a 'higher anointing,' you can expect a multiplied return." Then they will say, *"You know, Jesus said you will always have the poor with you . . ."* (John 12:8) implying that the poor aren't worth much, that they're a dime a dozen. This teaching is totally wrong and thoroughly unscriptural. Such suggestions are completely false interpretations of Proverbs 19:17 and John 12:8' (2000, pp.158,159). Hagan's attempt to correct the extremes was well placed, he addresses specific aberrant teachings and offers a clear and balanced Biblical correction.

Despite the potential for excess and imbalance, Hagan clearly believed in prosperity, he writes, 'I believe in prosperity. Yes, by that I do mean spiritual well-being and physical health. But I also mean material or financial blessing. When the Apostle John declared, *"Beloved, I wish above all things that thou mayest prosper and be in health, even as thy soul prospereth"* (3 John 2), I believe his intent and meaning was to refer to three distinct areas of life, material, physical, and spiritual' (2000, p.1).' Further, in his book 'The Midas Touch,' Hagin expounds on this verse specifically through the original Greek: 'Some people have argued that the phrase *"that thou mayest prosper"* does not refer to financial prosperity. They contend the phrase was nothing more than a common greeting, or idiom, of the day that simply meant, "May things go well for you." The Greek word translated "prosper" or "prospereth" in this text is "euodoo." Euodoo is comprised of the words "hodos," which means a road, and "eu," which means good. Thus, the Greek word eudoo (translated "prosper") literally means a good road or a good journey. So even if in this instance the word did not mean specifically to prosper financially, at the very least it meant to have a good and prosperous journey. I have a hard time understanding how anyone could have a good and prosperous journey if he didn't have adequate provisions for the trip, if he was broke, lacking, and in poverty and want every step of the way.' Hagin continues, 'Besides, this word translated "prosper" is the same Greek word the Apostle Paul used in First Corinthians 16:2 when he directed the believers in Corinth to set aside some money each week as God hath prospered him. Certainly, and without doubt, the word prosper can be and is used in Scripture in reference to financial prosperity' (2000: pp. 13,14).

Hagin as the unofficial leader of the 'Word of Faith' movement set about restoring Biblical balance to those colleagues who had gone off target. This ability to offer a circumspect assessment, demonstrates something that is constantly required within ministries, a willingness to recognize when things have gone wrong and to offer correction when an emphasis has been exaggerated. Regarding for example, those who have strayed in their understanding on returns for money sown, he observed: 'Feeling that they have been promised remarkable, extraordinary, and phenomenal returns, some have ended up disappointed and disillusioned when the result didn't materialize as they envisioned' (2000, p.126).

The 'Word of Faith' ministries, as religious organizations, are exempt from filing with the U.S. Internal Revenue Service. In 2007, U.S. Senator Charles Grassley, a member of the Senate Finance Committee, sent letters to six ministries about complaints he had received regarding non-independent boards and ministers' lavish lifestyles. The ministries included 'Word of Faith' ministers: Kenneth Copeland, Joyce Meyer and Creflo Dollar. On concluding the investigation in 2011 Grassley asked the Evangelical Council on Financial Accountability to study the issues and offer recommendations. The critics used this as leverage against the movement and there were aspects of sensationalism through the news media. What most people weren't aware of was that the same Senate Finance Committee, had also similarly investigated the affairs of the Smithsonian Museums, The Red Cross, American Universities and Non-profit hospitals, just to name a few. In other words, the investigations were not so unusual, and they ought not to have created such hysteria on certain news networks.

What appears to some as being a 'lavish lifestyle' is for another simply 'functional' necessities. A private jet aircraft for example, might well appear luxurious to some, but in function it is simply a means of private transportation. The ministries with private jet planes have an unusual and highly demanding schedule to keep. Often this schedule includes worldwide travel and it is therefore hardly surprising, that the chosen means of transportation is a private jet aircraft. The direction that the Bible gives regarding journeys is to have a prosperous one, *'Beloved, I wish above all things that thou mayest prosper and be in health, even as thy soul prospereth'* (3 John 2). As we have seen previously, this verse can especially be applied to transportation. Therefore, a luxurious ministry jet, is clearly more appropriate to a *'Prosperous journey'* than the restrictions and comparative discomfort of commercial travel. People who assess ministries, need to first appropriate an understanding of the impact on ministries, of their global networks. The Christian ministry has moved a long way on from the local parish. We have the internet, satellite television, mass communication, global transportation networks and jet aircraft. In effect, the world has shrunk and the 'Word of Faith' movement has been at the cutting edge of communication within these developing paradigms.

Further along these lines, it is also well worth noting that people such as the previously mentioned, Dillistone, have observed that theological doctrines can be influenced from the wider developments of a culture. He observed that as British law evolved within society during the Latin period this impacted theological doctrine, to the degree, that notions of 'Penal Substitution' evolved. Therefore, to some degree, we might consider that the 'Word of Faith' movement has been contextualized towards Biblical prosperity by the ongoing cultural influence of 'The American Dream.' Dillistone's historical observations could help critics understand why the 'Word of Faith' movement has been so successful and effective. However, the movement is not limited by this observation because its Biblical emphasis has proved to be supracultural, as shown in the previous examples from around the world.

In Ephesians 2:6 we read: *'And hath raised us up together and made us sit together in Heavenly places in Christ Jesus'* (Ephesians 2:6). From this Heavenly vantage point, looking down onto Earth, a new jet aircraft is not such a significant item. Of eternally more significance is a poor child, a grieving Mother, or a destitute and suicidal young man. The value we place on people and things, changes according to our vantage points in life. For the 'Word of Faith' movement, a jet plane or millions of dollars in resources are merely tools towards the work of the ministry. They provide the route to the goal, which is reaching people with the liberating Gospel message of Jesus Christ. Hagin's healthy emphasis summed things up well, 'We shouldn't be so concerned about getting sinners' money transferred into our hands. Our concern should be getting their hearts transferred into the Kingdom' (2000, p.141).

A further point that needs mentioning regarding finances, is that many medical reports and experts have highlighted the connection between worry,stress, and disease. It has been repeatedly observed that financial concerns are the number one causes of worry and stress for many people. Copeland has been clear, 'The gospel to the poor is that Jesus has come and they don't need to be poor anymore!' (1985, p.11). The links between poverty, worry, and the essential material goods of life were well understood by Jesus. Consequently, He taught believers: *'"Therefore do not worry, saying, 'What shall we eat?' or 'What shall we drink?' or 'What shall we wear?' 32 For after all these things the Gentiles seek. For your heavenly Father knows that you need all these things. 33 But seek first the kingdom of God and His righteousness, and all these things shall be added to you"'* (Matthew 6:31-33). In other words, Jesus Christ makes a direct promise to provide for those who follow Him, those who *'seek first the kingdom of God and His righteousness.'* Believing in these promises of provision alleviates stress and therefore, the potential sickness that is so often connected to it. As Copeland has observed, the Kingdom is affected by prosperity, otherwise 'it wouldn't produce *things*' (1985, p.13).

Having confidence in God's provision will also create excellent expectations. When Jesus for example, provided wine at the wedding feast in Cana, it was the best wine (John 2:1-11). Jesus provided a clear benchmark at this His first recorded public miracle; He provides the best. Therefore, it is entirely reasonable to expect that when He provides something for those who follow Him, they can expect the best. In promoting Biblical prosperity, the 'Word of Faith' movement has touched on this emphasis and also two other big issues of our times, worry and stress. These issues are significantly contributing to the breakdown of society and people are indulging in all manner of things to escape from them. Drugs, alcohol, and perversions of many kinds are being pursued in an attempt to escape from the pressures of worry and stress. Faith in the Gospel of Jesus Christ takes away the worry and stress, Jesus' words were given to combat these issues. Therefore, Biblical prosperity ought not to be seen as a frivolous doctrine or a selfish pursuit, but rather, something vital to a healthy individual life and subsequently of great importance to society as a whole.

Whilst many might not think that it is right for a minister to have financial wealth, the Bible offers no such limitations. However, there are many warnings regarding money, so the issue is a serious one but ultimately it is a heart issue. Each minister will need to make sure that they are not pursuing money first but rather the *'Kingdom of God.'* Hagin offered the 'Word of Faith' movement a list of priorities in giving. This list still applies to the authentic 'Word of Faith' movement today, he writes: 'I believe every believer should have a similar prioritized list of purposes for giving; such a list might look like this:

1) Because I love God
2) Because I want to obey God
3) Because I want to support the Great Commission and the Church
4) Because I want to see people blessed
5) Because I am planting seed for my own needs' (2000, p.121).

It should be well noted that for Hagin, his personal needs are positioned last in this list, his priority in giving was on loving and obeying God first.

Jesus Christ, teaching within the New Testament, speaks about the importance of giving specifically: *'Give, and it shall be given unto you; good measure, pressed down, and shaken together, and running over, shall men give into your bosom. For with the same measure that ye mete withal it shall be measured to you again'* (Luke 6:38). We can view many other texts that pertain to the blessings of God for believers. Ultimately, a picture builds up within the Bible that can be summarized from the wisdom of Proverbs, *'The blessing of the Lord maketh rich, and He addeth no sorrow with it'* (Proverbs 10:22). The Bible is clear, God wants to bless his children in all ways, providing for their complete prosperity which includes finances.

However, many people miss out on *'the blessing of the Lord'* because they have become focussed on the many warnings within the Bible regarding money. Often, the 'Word of Faith' movement has not engaged fully with these warnings, there has been an imbalance of emphasis at times. The Bible gives clear warning regarding the pursuit of money, the love of money, the greed for money, trusting in money and many other warnings. Consider for example this clear warning from the Apostle Paul: *'Perverse disputings of men of corrupt minds, and destitute of the truth, supposing that gain is godliness: from such withdraw thyself.6 But godliness with contentment is great gain.7 For we brought nothing into this world, and it is certain we can carry nothing out.8 And having food and raiment let us be therewith content.9 But they that will be rich fall into temptation and a snare, and into many foolish and hurtful lusts, which drown men in destruction and perdition.10 For the love of money is the root of all evil: which while some coveted after, they have erred from the faith, and pierced themselves through with many sorrows'* (1 Timothy 6:5-10). Prosperity critics often focus on verses such as these above all others. However, the key is found in balance. The pull of financial wealth and riches is great. Believers, therefore, need to focus on a discipled life, with the focus being firmly on God, above all else.

Context is a vital key in understanding the Bible. In the previous chapter of 1 Timothy mentioned above for example, the Apostle has taught that certain diligent ministers are worthy of double honour. In the Greek, the word for honour is transliterated 'timé,' which meant a valuing, a price, it was equated with money (1 Timothy 5:17,18). Therefore, whilst there are warnings in chapter 6 regarding finances, in chapter 5 double financial blessing was deemed appropriate for certain ministers. Further, the Apostle clearly taught about sowing and reaping financially. Let's read from 2 Corinthians 9 verses 6-8: *'But this I say: He who sows sparingly will also reap sparingly, and he who sows bountifully will also reap bountifully. 7 So let each one give as he purposes in his heart, not grudgingly or of necessity; for God loves a cheerful giver. 8 And God is able to make all grace abound toward you, that you, always having all sufficiency in all things, may have an abundance for every good work.'* Clearly, here the Apostle is encouraging people towards reaping bountifully so that they will have an abundant supply.

Some people see a dichotomy in the Apostle Paul's writing between the blessing of God regarding financial prosperity and the warnings about money. In truth, there isn't a dichotomy, there is rather a need for wisdom and balance. The issue for many of the critics of Biblical prosperity, is that they haven't differentiated between the negative love of money and the positive use of money.

The warnings of the bible regarding money are orientated around money being the focus of a person's desires and ambitions. When God remains the focus of a person's desires and ambitions, they can then be free to accept, believe, and walk in prosperity. The old adage of, 'Having money and making sure that money doesn't have you,' is a good summary of this position. Jesus was very clear in promising all the goods of life to believers, the condition being that they put the *'Kingdom of God'* and *'His righteousness'* first place in their lives. (Matthew 6:33).

Some people have an issue with the extent of lavish lifestyle that some ministers seem to enjoy. I knew a businessman for example, who denied himself any luxury because he wanted to use all the proceeds of his business, to pay for operations for poor people in Africa. In the end, the pressure he put himself under made his life miserable. Finally, he couldn't continue any further and sought God in prayer, it was only then that he found release. He sensed God direct him to give as the Bible instructs and the Holy Spirit leads. After this was done, he would be free to spend the rest of his finances however he desired. He could buy cars, watches, houses, whatever he chose, in the freedom of knowing that he was entirely in God's will. We read in Proverbs 24 verses 3 and 4 for example: *'Through wisdom is an house builded; and by understanding it is established: 4 And by knowledge shall the chambers be filled with all precious and pleasant riches.'* Clearly, if we regard the Bible's instruction *'precious and pleasant riches'* are entirely acceptable. The key for the believer is not to focus on *'precious and pleasant riches'* but rather to focus on the will of God.

Steven Lyn Evans

Healing & troubles

The 'Word of Faith' movement like many others, has promoted Biblical healing. This is an area where there are potential issues and misunderstanding at times. For the 'Word of Faith' movement healing can be seen clearly in 1 Peter 2:24 and here in Isaiah 53, where Jesus' future life on Earth was foretold in the clearest of terms: *'Surely he hath borne our griefs, and carried our sorrows: yet we did esteem him stricken, smitten of God, and afflicted. But he was wounded for our transgressions, he was bruised for our iniquities: the chastisement of our peace was upon him; and with his stripes we are healed'* (Isaiah 53:4,5).

In the Gospel of Matthew, it is understood that Isaiah's description of this healing ministry was found in Jesus Christ, *'That it might be fulfilled which was spoken by Esaias the prophet, saying, Himself took our infirmities, and bare our sicknesses'* (Matthew 8:17). The word *'Infirmity'* here in the original Greek means without strength, an ailment that deprives a person of doing what they would like to do. The word for *'Disease'* in the Greek, pertains to that which is a chronic persisting disease and something that is often incurable. Matthew understands that through Jesus this healing flows. Further, individual faith facilitates healing and Matthew also records Jesus words to the Roman centurion, *'Go thy way; and as thou hast believed, so be it done unto thee'* (Matthew 8:13). Later, in the Gospel Jesus teaches, *'And all things, whatsoever ye shall ask in prayer, believing, ye shall receive'* (Matthew 21:22). The New Testament is therefore very clear in teaching healing for believers and the 'Word of Faith' movement have promoted these Biblical promises. This robust Biblical position, as we have seen within this work, has been a great blessing for many within the 'Word of Faith' movement.

However, at times, because of this emphasis, when tragedy or trouble comes, the movement appears to have struggled to lend support to those dealing with difficult situations. McConnell has picked up on this and noted that there seems to be a lack of counseling for those who are sick and needy (1988, p.164). Furthermore, McConnell has also suggested that 'faith churches have little or no concept of Pastoral care for the chronically and terminally ill believer.' McConnell goes on to suggest that the sick believer is shunned within the movement and regarded with suspicion because believers ought not to be sick due to the provision for healing within the Atonement (1988, p.165). Despite the many difficulties in answering these anecdotal generalizations, the 'Word of Faith' movement could make a self-assessment and consider how believers respond to those in need. It should also be noted that these apparent weaknesses, are due in part, to an expectation that God's will is healing. There isn't a theology of sickness within the New Testament but there is a strong theology of healing. There is a difference of pastoral emphasis within the movement in comparison to other groups or denominations and this has been because a great number of its members have been healed. We have viewed the testimony of Dodi Osteen earlier; this is as an example that has inspired many within the movement to believe for their healing. This supernatural emphasis has caused a different approach and expectation. Therefore, any potential weaknesses in these areas need to be addressed, without undermining faith for healing. Walking in love is a key emphasis within the 'Word of Faith' movement, the outworking of this, will further help meet these pastoral issues.

In addition, the movement has at times, been too silent on what to do for those in tragic circumstances. For these people, a double burden hits them. Firstly, the tragedy itself and then the perceived failure of their faith, both are difficult to process. The Perriman Report has concluded that there seems to be a pressure that exists within the 'Word of Faith' movement, to conceal anything that resembles a failure of faith (2003, p.233). Several of the 'Word of Faith' people I have counseled over the years, have testified that when some trouble happened in their lives they felt as though it ought not to have happened. The reality of what they were experiencing was outside of their Biblical framework of reference. They were subsequently unable to process the situation. This has been a weakness, knowing how to support people in the midst of tragedy is an important pastoral issue. Further, when some peoples experience doesn't match with their Biblical expectations, if they don't have the wisdom to process the situation, the disappointment can break their Biblical framework for life. Some people have even appeared to have given up on believing as a result of this. However, this situation is due to the movement's members not aligning themselves with a fuller Biblical understanding, rather than anything the 'Word of Faith' movement has specifically done.

The strength of the 'Word of Faith' movement, is that it employs a position of belief in the Biblical promises but when the expectation doesn't match the reality, the movement has often been silent. The unspoken equation in such circumstances, results in a conclusion that faith wasn't employed, or faith wasn't big enough. That puts responsibility and even a feeling of liability on the one suffering, in sometimes tragic circumstances. At times, I have been told that people have felt as if they were 'not cared for,' 'left behind,' and even 'ignored.' The 'Word of Faith' movement's beliefs ought not to cause any difficulty to those facing tragedy or a perceived defeat in life. Rather, the tragic circumstances can be met with encouragement and support. The fellowship of kind, biblically illuminating, faith building conversations, can contribute greatly towards processing tragic circumstances.

In explaining Biblical absolutes, the 'Word of Faith' movement could commit too engaging in something along the lines of the following. This would help people process the situations they face with a Biblical perspective. Firstly, we can recognize that tragedy and bad things happen for multiple reasons:

Reasons for troubles in life

1) Troubles can be an attack of Satan whose focus is to steal, kill, and destroy (John 10:10).
2) Troubles can be caused by bad choices (Acts 5:1,2).
3) Troubles can come from the sinful nature (James 4:1-10).
4) Troubles can come through the forces of nature that have been corrupted because sin entered the earth (Matthew 24:7).
5) Troubles ought not to be a surprise, Jesus taught that: *'Sufficient unto the day is the evil thereof'* (Matthew 6:34b).

What to emphasize when troubles come

1) The love of God. Satan attacks the love of God, he entices people to question it, as part of his plan to discourage and defeat them.
2) When tragedies happen, it is not a judgment of God in order to teach something.
3) God put our sin, sickness, disease, sorrow, grief and poverty on Jesus when He was crucified, in order to redeem us.
4) God always turns our situation around for His good: *'And we know that all things work together for good to them that love God, to them who are the called according to his purpose'* (Romans 8:28).
5) God has given us His Word and the Holy Spirit to teach us (John 14:26, 16:13) (2 Timothy 3:16-17).
6) Jesus said He came to destroy the works of the devil and to bring abundant life (John 10:10).

7) Regardless to what has happened, Isaiah 54:17 says, *'No weapon formed against you shall prosper!'*
8) Ultimately, we must keep focused on the promises of God: In Romans we read the following excellent summary: *'Who shall separate us from the love of Christ? shall tribulation, or distress, or persecution, or famine, or nakedness, or peril, or sword? 36 As it is written, For thy sake we are killed all the day long; we are accounted as sheep for the slaughter. 37 Nay, in all these things we are more than conquerors through him that loved us. 38 For I am persuaded, that neither death, nor life, nor angels, nor principalities, nor powers, nor things present, nor things to come, 39 Nor height, nor depth, nor any other creature, shall be able to separate us from the love of God, which is in Christ Jesus our Lord'* (Romans 8:35-39).

Relationships & presumption

Another area of potential improvement for the 'Word of Faith' movement is in the relationships between ministers and churches from outside the movement. It's worth mentioning that the critics' mythology has at times, contributed to suspicion, and subsequent communication difficulties between 'Word of Faith' ministries and other believers. Understandably, some 'Word of Faith' ministries have been cautious and a self-protecting distance, has on occasion, contributed to the perpetuation of suspicion.

In the main, the 'Word of Faith' movement has chosen not to engage with the mythology creators. Partly, this has been because the critics' claims have often not warranted attention. Whilst not engaging with the critics has often been a wise strategy for the 'Word of Faith' movement, there have been ministers who have taken the silent approach too far and applied that strategy to other believers when disagreements have arisen. There is some anecdotal evidence of a culture of silence at times, within the 'Word of Faith' movement. Some belong to one group, some another, unless divisions are addressed, this can lead to subtle but definite issues. One group of people emphasized their college over all others and a 'spiritual snobbery' has evolved at times. In such cases, a lack of words can potentially cause more injury than well intentioned words would. I recall the example of a 'Word of Faith' minister who cut off all ties with another ministry, without any explanation. He then subsequently denied all communication. The pain of this refusal to communicate was both an abuse of trust and of our calling to walk in love. In misunderstanding the difference between positive and negative words, this minister thought he should avoid all potentially negative appearing words. In the process, the lack of words caused dissension and several unnecessary ongoing issues for those involved. The Bible teaches ministers to speak the truth in love, so that we can *'grow up in all things into Him who is the head, Christ'* (Ephesians 4:15). Further, the New Testament gives us the charge to *'Preach the word; be instant in season, out of season; reprove, rebuke, exhort with all longsuffering and doctrine'* (2 Timothy 4:2). In doing this, the 'Word of Faith' movement can rescue some people and help others not to be led astray by the critics' mythology, or other misunderstandings. The book of 2 Peter explains it this way, *'Ye therefore, beloved, seeing ye know these things before, beware lest ye also, being led away with the error of the wicked, fall from your own stedfastness'* (2 Peter 3:17). The call to engage our efforts and communication towards truth is clear.

Further, the cynical cessationists and mythology creators who have attacked the 'Word of Faith' movement, ought not to go unchallenged. Their position is utterly indefensible, unbiblical, and treats the Biblical charge of Jesus Christ for believers with contempt. Jesus clearly taught, *"And these signs will follow those who believe: In My name they will cast out demons; they will speak with new tongues; ...they will lay hands on the sick, and they will recover"* (Mark 16:17,18b). Despite any Biblical evidence those who attack the 'Word of Faith' movement have the temerity to denounce Jesus' words as being limited to the Apostolic age only. They deny significantly large portions of the Bible, millions of believers' testimonies throughout the ages, and the ongoing work of the Holy Spirit for believers today. They denounce people who are filled with the Holy Spirit, people who laugh, dance, speak in tongues and have all the signs associated with the Day of Pentecost itself. The Bible teaches us that to denounce the move and work of the Holy Spirit is the most serious of errors: *'And anyone who speaks a word against the Son of Man, it will be forgiven him; but to him who blasphemes against the Holy Spirit, it will not be forgiven'* (Luke 12:10). According to Strong's Concordance blasphemy properly means, a refusal to acknowledge that which is good and worthy of respect. Hence to blaspheme is slander, it is to speak lightly or profanely of sacred things such as the operation and manifestation of the Holy Spirit. Therefore, if someone is genuinely laughing with joy in the Holy Spirit, speaking in tongues, or doing anything else under the Holy Spirit's influence, those who criticize them for that manifestation are potentially blaspheming the Holy Spirit.

Word of Faith

The seriousness of this issue demands a response at times. However, the 'Word of Faith' movement has often been overly gentle and even passive in responding to its critics. A more robust response would often potentially be of great benefit to some, who might otherwise be led astray by the critics. The critics have mocked the manifestations of the Holy Spirit and have positioned themselves as a sort of 'spiritual police-force.' Their error is plain enough but to those with little understanding or discernment, they can be pulled by the tide of scoffing compromise.

At times, there has been an independent culture within the 'Word of Faith' movement. In many ways, this has been healthy and has helped the movement advance, the Bible teaches that: *'...each one's work will become clear'* (1 Corinthians 3:13). Also, *'But let each one examine his own work, and then he will have rejoicing in himself alone, and not in another. 5 For each one shall bear his own load'* (Galatians 6:4,5). These scriptures highlight the importance of an individual's ministry. However, the individual emphasis between ministers and ministries ought not to lead to isolation.

On occasion, 'Word of Faith' movement ministries have tended to distance themselves from other believers and an individualistic emphasis has emerged. Partly, this has been due to protectionism which has been necessary to avoid the potentially corrupting influence of liberal voices. However, in the future, the movement could look to further its influence into other church networks. The many dwindling denominations within western society have congregations, who might often be delighted to have their lives impacted, by the influence of an enthusiastic 'Word of Faith' minister.

Conclusion

Breaking through human limitations

Have you heard the expression 'an elephant never forgets?' Well, perhaps it's not always a good thing, at times the ability to forget can be a tremendous asset. Are there things that you need to forget? Are there invisible boundaries that you have placed in your own mind? Many people are limited by their own understanding and past experiences in life. Let me share an illustration with you: Whenever a baby elephant is born in captivity, the owners know that training must be provided early, if it is the elephant will be obedient and easier to handle in the subsequent years. Baby elephants are inquisitive creatures, they want to walk around and explore their environment, the owners however when training the elephants, restrict this exploration by placing a chain around one of the legs. The chain is then connected to a large stake, which is driven deep into the ground. The baby elephants walk around in the small area provided by whatever slack in the chain there might be. It can be a sad sight to see them straining, and pulling, in a vain attempt to break free from the chain.

By the time the elephant is fully-grown, the chains around the leg have been replaced. I want to invite you now, to ask yourself the question, by what? Take a minute and consider, if a baby elephant needed a chain and large stake, what might the massive fully-grown animal require? Perhaps a larger heavier chain and stake? Or several chains and stakes? No, not at all, the answer is remarkable, a mere rope and stick! Yes, that's right, a mere rope and stick! The elephant has been restricted for so long by the chains during its formative years, that whenever it feels the tug of the rope as an adult, it simply retreats backward and doesn't even attempt to pull free. It has been conditioned to the limits and restrictions of the chain. Despite its immense power to easily break free and snap the rope, it remains frustrated, within a very limited space. The limitations of the past have determined the elephant's behavior in the present.

For many people their lives might be compared to that elephant, they live trapped, within the very limited space of their experience and human rationale. This is where the mythology peddlers, critics and especially the heretical cessationists are located. They think that they are unable to break free because their experience has taught them to accept a restricted life. The limitations, restrictions, and often disappointments of the past, have determined their behavior and beliefs in the present. They have grown to expect and teach out of this anti-supernatural perspective. However Christian living is not meant to be like this, Jesus promised *'I am come that they might have life, and that they might have it more abundantly'* (John 10:10b). Like the elephant, we have immense power to snap any ropes of limitation and bondage. The Gospel of Jesus Christ has provided this, the only question is, will we truly believe the Gospel and use the power that is available to us? The 'Word of Faith' movement has accepted the supernatural mandate of the New Covenant. The cessationists and mythology promoters are not only staying within the limits of their experiences, they are vigorously opposing anyone who desires Biblical supernatural experiences. In so doing, they are driving in the poles of doubt and multiplying the chains of bondage.

In its important conclusion, the Perriman Report argues that there is enough common ground for 'rapprochement between the 'Word of Faith' movement and the more mainstream evangelical church' (2003, p.230). The conclusions of this significant and academic report are clearly at odds with the mythology of the critics. Therefore, the proof is clear, the attacks against the 'Word of Faith' movement are out of balance with the leading and authoritative academic analysis.

Within this work we have shown definitive proofs that provide us with important conclusive evidence.

It has been shown that:

1) Kenyon wasn't the movements father, although he is an influential figure.
2) Kenyon didn't have links with metaphysical cults.
3) There are no metaphysical influences on the 'Word of Faith' movement.
4) The 'Word of Faith' movement's theology isn't cultic.

5) Kenneth Hagin is the father of the 'Word of Faith' movement.
6) The 'Word of Faith' atonement doctrine has been shown to be a mixture of the three orthodox historical atonement doctrines.
7) The 'Word of Faith' movement employs a Biblical theology.
8) The 'Word of Faith' movement continues an ancient line of believers who experience tongues, healing, miracles, and other supernatural experiences such as exorcisms.
9) The 'Word of Faith' movement is a significant worldwide move of God.
10) McConnell developed a mythology regarding the 'Word of Faith' movement.
11) McConnell, MacArthur, Hanegraaff, Hunt and Peters, along with the other critics, have often used their mythology to justify attacks against the 'Word of Faith' movement.
12) The critics often hold to the heresy of cessationism.
13) The critics of the 'Word of Faith' movement have facilitated liberalism.
14) The 'Word of Faith' critics have created serious and unnecessary divisions within the church.
15) The critics are almost always rooted in the limits of Enlightenment influenced western theology.

Further observations from our conclusions

1) Many critics of the 'Word of Faith' movement have a cessationist position. People such as McConnell, Peters, Hunt and MacArthur who wrote 'Charismatic Chaos' in 1993, have perpetually criticized the 'Word of Faith' movement. The cessationist position denies the Biblical truth and believes that spiritual gifts such as speaking in tongues, prophecy, and healing ceased with the apostolic age. These positions are heretical. They reject Jesus' commission and large sections of the Bible which teaches that supernatural events will follow those who believe.
2) Other critics are not cessationists but have displayed an ongoing skepticism towards supernatural gifts. They have been supported by the Enlightenment rooted western theological emphasis, which is generally skeptical of the supernatural.
3) Many of the critics have exhibited a pathological desire to attack the movement, to the degree that they have embraced an

inaccurate, unbalanced, history and theology. This has resulted in acutely inaccurate conclusions being made to support the mythology.

4) People such as Dillistone have observed that many theological doctrines have evolved from the wider developments of a culture. We saw that British law for example, which evolved within society during the Latin period, impacted theological doctrine such, that notions of 'Penal Substitution' developed. The 'Word of Faith' movement's roots developed from post-World War II hopefulness and at times, they can be seen as reflecting aspects of 'The American Dream.'

5) The movement, like all movements, is not without issues and these must be taken seriously. Hagin took care to address certain financial issues and imbalances in his book 'The Midas Touch.' Moving forward, the movement can consider potential development in understanding issues such as those cited in chapter 10.

6) The western theological anti-supernatural emphasis, born from the Enlightenment's Critical Theory, offers a biased and restrictive worldview. In its extremes, this view has led to the heresy of cessationist theology, seen in many critics of the 'Word of Faith' movement such as MacArthur, Hunt and Peters. Western theological skepticism towards the supernatural has robbed people from understanding legitimate Biblical spirituality. Consequently, to some degree, whilst western denominational church numbers are often hemorrhaging, rapid growth is taking place within other groups such as the New Age movement, Witchcraft and Wicca.

Here we present 12 vital focuses that have contributed towards the success of the 'Word of Faith' movement:

- The worship of God.
- A quality decision to walk in faith and love.
- The Word of God as an authoritative foundation for life.
- Prayers of faith and tongues of various kinds.
- Faith is expressed in human words.
- Believers experience the supernatural life of the Kingdom.
- Being a new creation in Christ.
- Salvation and healing are found within the atonement.

- Living in the blessing: Prosperity of spirit, soul, (mind, will and emotions) and body.
- Biblical truth should direct believers not emotions and feelings.
- A refusal to ask people for money.
- A refusal to ask people for places to minister and instead a prayerful reliance on God to open up opportunities.

Since McConnell's thesis in 1982, there have been tremendous changes within the Christian church. The liberal and secular advancement has impacted the denominational churches who have seen their numbers hemorrhaging. With all the difficulties that have been going on, the 'Word of Faith' movement's critics, have attacked one of the most prominent and growing global Christian movements.

There is a crisis in Christianity, and it has been largely ignored by the critics of the 'Word of Faith' movement. The crisis is the radical growth of liberal and secular trends formulating within the so-called 'church.' The critics have chosen to use their resources to create a mythology and attack the 'Word of Faith' movement. These same critics have been mostly silent on the real crisis of liberalism and secularism that is attacking the church. They have missed the real issues that the church faces and embraced the illegitimate anti-Biblical mythology. In misdirecting their efforts, they have left the way open for the growth of secular and liberal perspectives to influence the church.

The mythology created by McConnell and adopted by the subsequent critics has had severely negative implications. This does put into question the real impetus behind the critics, if they are so concerned with truth, why are they so silent in the face of the radically secular and liberal voices? If they are so concerned with heresy, why are they silent in the face of the loudest and most obvious voices of heresy? Further, we have shown that a great irony exists, in that many of the critics of the 'Word of Faith' movement are firmly committed to the heresy of cessationism. It was shown that this position goes against established church history, Biblical teaching, and the reality of modern church life, this is a dangerous heresy. In effect, the critics such as McConnell, John MacArthur, Dave Hunt and Justin Peters for example, have attempted to advocate for disbelief in the Bible and Jesus Christ's charge to believers, to minister in supernatural works. This position is without any scriptural support. McConnell, MacArthur, Peters, Hunt and the other critics are joined in their cessationism by groups such as the Jehovah's Witnesses and Mormonism.

There is a clear supernatural heritage of Christians throughout the ages. These leaders have shown us a true and Biblical expectation of miracles, healing, and the essential supernatural dimensions of the Christian life. Included in this heritage we first cited some of the Biblical examples and then people such as: Justyn Martyr, Irenaeus, Polycarp, Tertullian, Gregory the 'Wonder Worker,' Augustine, Luther, Calvin, Wesley, Spurgeon, and many more modern examples. The critics have ignored the obvious correlation between the supernatural emphasis of Christian leaders of the past, and the modern leaders of the Christian world, many of whom are from the 'Word of Faith' movement. The movement is not only transcultural but has proved that when the mission has a Biblical emphasis, it can be supra-cultural, and the emphasis is therefore universally valid.

Within this work we have had a commitment towards theology being rooted in real life, for this reason it was vital to have included supernatural examples and testimonies. This approach is more Eastern, holistic, and Biblical, it should be differentiated from the linear Platonistic approach of much within modern Enlightenment based western theology. Further, some of the examples and testimonies included within this work prove the important missiological observation that, 'Miraculous physical healing does exactly what the Enlightenment says cannot be done' (2005, p.151). The 'Word of Faith' movement has often not been understood because the critics' theological framework is significantly limited by Enlightenment based theological rationale.

Progressing to prosperity

The Perriman Report quotes Moo who suggests that the 'Word of Faith' movement are 'justified in criticizing the church in the west for too often unintentionally fostering an unbiblical anthropological dualism by confining God's concerns to the human soul' (2003, pp. 220-221). Following on from this, the report also mentions Gammons' ironic observation, that the 'fiercest critics of prosperity teaching are the prosperous middle-class churches.' The report also recognizes that there is force to Copeland's argument that one of the main reasons why 'we've never won the world to Jesus is that we've never shown them how God could help them deal with the material monster that's eating them alive right now. Instead, we've acted like God was so far above material things that He wouldn't have anything to do with them (2003, p.221). These observations contribute towards an understanding that the 'Word of Faith' movement 'constitutes an extension of the Pentecostal/charismatic challenge to evangelicalism which has become over-intellectualized, sanitized, reduced to something altogether too tame and ineffectual' (2003, p.218).

So many people don't allow their thinking to change, they remain entrenched in the limits of their past experiences and the limits of human rationale. I recall, many years ago now, being told by my evangelist friend Martin Newman, about a friend of his called Jimmy. Jimmy, like my friend Martin, was originally from Dublin in Ireland but had moved to London in the 1950's looking for work. He was a small man, less than five feet tall and for work he would sell the London Evening Standard Newspaper on the street corners. Money was always tight and often Jimmy would save money on accommodation by digging out a hole in the grounds of Green Park, or one of the other public parks in London. He would then line the hole with lots of old newspapers, cover himself with leaves, and go to sleep under the stars, free of charge! Martin, on the other hand, had made a financial success of his life. He was a wealthy property developer and entrepreneur. He'd always remained good pals with his fellow 'Dubliner' and when time allowed, he would collect his friend from his newspaper stand and they would enjoy a bit of time together.

One day Martin drove up to collect Jimmy in a beautiful new Jaguar convertible car. Jimmy sunk into the plush leather vehicle with a beaming smile, and they drove off to a top London Hotel in Kensington for lunch. Whilst there in the VIP lounge, they found themselves sitting alongside some well-known showbiz people of that time. There was Robert Plant, the singer from the group Led Zeppelin, Gloria Gaynor the disco and gospel singer was also there, and the actor Dudley Moore with his wife. It was a happy and very friendly afternoon, and it wasn't long before Jimmy was the centre of attention. Jimmy was playing the spoons on his knees, on his elbows, and even his head, while conducting the singing of the Our Father! His famous audience was enthralled by him, they wanted to know about his life, where he was from and where he lived, etc. When he told them about sleeping in the parks, they were shocked, and Dudley Moore kindly said that as he had a mansion in Buckinghamshire with plenty of spare bedrooms, Jimmy could go back with him and be his guest.

When they left the Hotel that evening, Martin said he could barely see the top of Jimmy's little head as he waved goodbye from the back of Dudley Moore's Rolls Royce. On arriving at the beautiful mansion, the instructions given to the Butler by Mr. Moore were very clear, he was told to look after Jimmy, to make sure that he was comfortable in the guest suite, and to give him anything that he wanted.

In the morning, Dudley Moore and his wife were woken up by the Butler's frantic knocking on their bedroom door: *"Mr. Moore, Mr. Moore, your guest has disappeared, I've searched everywhere for him he hasn't slept in his bed, he's nowhere to be found, what should I do?"* Dudley Moore, his wife and the Butler, all went into the guest suite to look for Jimmy, they looked under the four-poster bed, on top of the four-poster bed, in the cupboards, the en-suite bathroom, the living room, everywhere. Then Mrs. Moore, who was looking behind the curtains, looked through the window into the autumn, golden leafy garden, and there was Jimmy! He had dug a hole in the ground, covered it in leaves and slept there the previous night! What a situation! Jimmy had been given the best the world has to offer, but he refused it. Instead, he crept back into a hole in the ground!

What a strange thing to do, it just didn't make sense, why would Jimmy have done this? Well, Jimmy did what many people do, he just retreated to what he had grown to know best. Despite the greatness of what was on offer to him, the comfort of what is familiar proved to be the enemy of his blessing.

Many people are doing precisely the same thing as Jimmy with the opportunities they've been given as members of the family of God. They've been offered the *'riches of His grace,'* but they've not accepted what's on offer. Often, they aren't even aware of what's on offer, they live ignorant of their great position and potential in Christ. Clearly, there is a need in every Christian to apply themselves towards Bible study. However, the study of the Bible ought not to be done in a merely academic manner. The Bible is an ancient and supernatural book, the words contained in it offer spiritual guidance and can impact into both the spiritual and physical realms. This is how we are transformed through the Word of God; the Apostle Paul wrote of this: *'Study to shew thyself approved unto God, a workman that needeth not to be ashamed, rightly dividing the word of truth'* (2 Timothy 2:15). Western theology is usually lacking in its ability to process Biblical truth to a level of devotional acceptance. Enlightenment based notions of Critical Theory have often systematically robbed people of this ability.

The Bible shows repeatedly, there is an emphasis on prosperity for the believer. There are many scriptures that promise this, and in many ways the entire Bible is about blessings for those who follow God. Joshua puts it this way: *'This Book of the Law shall not depart from your mouth, but you shall meditate in it day and night, that you may observe to do according to all that is written in it. For then you will make your way prosperous, and then you will have good success'* (Joshua 1:8). The spiritual walk of yielding to Biblical truth and being an instrument of positive change, is a route less trod. Within this, there exists another irony of the Kingdom, the prosperity deniers have adopted a carnal position and the believers in prosperity are being led by the Spirit and Word of God.

The lack of money needs to be clearly seen as an instrument of stress, sickness and disease. Medical professionals have recognized that stress can cause disease and the number one reason for stress in the world is financial lack. So much of the world aches with lack, it is irresponsible for believers not to believe that God can use them, to combat this by prospering them. As Copeland phrases it, 'Blessed to be a blessing.' This summarizes a healthy attitude for believers. In understanding money positively, people can enter a wealthy mentality and become givers, encouragers, and sowers in the Kingdom of God.

A global move of God

Within this work, we have uncovered the most serious of issues relating to the critics of the 'Word of Faith' movement. We have shown that in their blinkered desire to attack the movement, they have created a mythology.

The critics have almost entirely come from western, Enlightenment based, theological trends. We noted the bizarre reality of this in the critics' silence towards radical liberalism and the acceptance of people such as Bultmann. We saw this juxtaposed to the rejection of Biblical advocates such as Hagin and Copeland. The hypocrisy of this situation should be considered as both obvious and unacceptable. We have also seen the heresy of the cessationists who have been supported by other critics against the 'Word of Faith' movement. Western theology has often been blinded by the Enlightenment and the results have had a devastating impact on western Christianity. We noted Christian anthropologist Charles Kraft's observation that western theological analysis is bound to exclusively Western methodologies and is entirely different to the methods employed by the majority of the rest of the world (1996:88). These methodologies can be traced back to the Enlightenment and Kraft suggests correctly that 'mission practice requires more Spirit-power based behavior' (1996:211).

Surely, it is time for the critics to leave the confines of limiting western theology and embrace a more expansive and Biblical global reality. This reality can be seen within the global ministries of the 'Word of Faith' movement. For the believer in Jesus Christ surely this is essential, Christ commissioned believers to: *"Go into all the world and preach the gospel to all creation"* (Mark 16:15).

The empirical evidence is clear, 'Word of Faith' movement has been a great move of God for our times. Like all the moves of God historically, it has had some highly vocal critics. Nevertheless, the 'Word of Faith' movement continues to flourish and to lead many people around the world, into the fullness of salvation through the Gospel of Jesus Christ. The movement has further helped spearhead the truth about prosperity, healing, and the supernatural life of Christians. These are vital truths for a suffering world that is impoverished, sick, and defeated, without the Gospel of Jesus Christ.

We conclude with the words of the Apostle Paul to the Ephesian church, in the hope that believers might walk together in a worthy way: '*I therefore, the prisoner of the Lord, beseech you that ye walk worthy of the vocation wherewith ye are called, With all lowliness and meekness, with longsuffering, forbearing one another in love; Endeavouring to keep the unity of the Spirit in the bond of peace. There is one body, and one Spirit, even as ye are called in one hope of your calling; One Lord, one faith, one baptism, One God and Father of all, who is above all, and through all, and in you all*' (Ephesians 4:1-6).

Receiving the Nicklaus' Founders Trophy, from course designer, and P.G.A. Player Gary Nicklaus, along with B.B.C. Sports Presenter Jason Mohammed (See pages 97-99)

Being able to visualize and then believing and speaking words of faith will impact on every aspect of your life!

Some of the headlines from the press in the U.K.

The power of God impacting people lives!

Names and Subject Index

A

AFCM 27
Anglicanism 75
Anselm of Canterbury 80
Apostle Paul xvi, 18, 33, 122, 126–127, 142, 144
Apostles Creed 79–80
Aquinas, Thomas 44, 81
Assemblies of God 27, 62
Atonement 6, 12–14, 18–20, 26, 40, 42, 47, 50, 66–67, 74, 76–78, 80–89, 92, 104, 128, 137–138
Augustine, Saint 13
Aulén, Bishop Gustaf 12, 74, 78–81, 84–87

B

Banks, Melvin xi, xviii,
Bethel Bible College 25
Bonaventure 45
Bosch, David 2, 41, 43–44, 94, 111
Bowler, Kate 16
Bowman, Robert 8, 10, 24–26, 55, 63, 68–69, 72–73, 75–76, 87, 89, 103, 116–117

Branham, William 51
Broadhead, Edwin K. 5
Brown, Bishop Tom x, xi, 105
Bultman, Rudolf 4, 143
Burkett 46

C

Calvinistic 58
Calvin, John 47–48, 80, 88, 140
Capitalism 39
Capitalistic 39
Capps, Charles xiv, xvii, 53
Caricatures 8, 19
Cartwright, Peter 61
Cessationism xviii, 1–3, 5–7, 9, 12, 16, 22, 28, 50, 54–55, 57–59, 70–71, 87, 94, 111–113, 115–116, 132, 136–139, 143
Cessationists 22, 55, 57–58, 70, 94, 112–113, 115–116, 137
Characterizations 22, 75, 82
Charismatic 1, 9, 11, 14, 16, 25, 46–47, 51, 61, 71, 75, 81, 107, 137, 141
Christ ix–x, xiv, xviii, 6, 12, 17–18, 22, 26, 28, 34, 40–43,

147

45–47, 49–51, 53, 56, 60–61, 67, 69, 75, 78–81, 84–92, 94, 99–100, 102, 106–109, 113, 115, 118, 121, 124–126, 128, 131–132, 136–139, 142–144
Christian Science 17, 67–68, 114, 117
Christus Victor 12, 79
Coleman, Simon 38
Context 12, 24, 32–33, 43, 64, 68–69, 75, 110–112, 126
Contextualization 28, 107–110
Copeland, Kenneth ix, xiv, xvii, 5, 8, 11, 19, 22–24, 26, 29–33, 35–47, 50–53, 55, 62, 72, 75–76, 83, 89–90, 94, 99, 105, 108–109, 117, 119–121, 123–124, 140, 143
Correlation Method 39
Cotterell, Peter 93
Critical Theory xiv, xvii, 71, 138, 142
Cullis, C. 68
Cultic 6, 8, 11, 13–17, 19, 24, 26, 47, 54, 63, 65, 70–71, 76, 114, 116–117, 136
Cyprianic 59

D

Dark Ages 45
DeArteaga, William 6, 8–10, 19, 47, 54, 64, 66, 68–71, 75, 77, 80, 84, 86–87
Demons 9, 53, 55–57, 103, 113, 115, 132
Descartes, René 94
Dillistone, F. W. 78, 124, 138
Doctrines 8–9, 12, 15–17, 19–20, 45–46, 61, 66–67, 71, 73–78, 81, 83–87, 92, 117, 124, 137–138
Dollar, Creflo xiv, xvii, 52–53, 123
Duplantis, Jesse xiv, 22–24, 52–53

E

Eastern Orthodox Church 6, 20, 77, 100
Economics 39
Eddy, Mary Baker 114
Emerson College of Oratory 25, 68
Enlightenment xiv, xvii, 2–5, 28, 43, 71, 82, 93–94, 101, 111–112, 121, 137, 140, 142–143

F

Farah, Charles 61, 63, 119
Fiat Money 141
Fillmore, Charles 70
Finney, Charles G. 47, 61
Franciscans 45
Free Will Baptist 25, 69, 72
From the Pinnacle of the Temple 63, 119

G

Gilliland, D. 107
God vii, ix–xi, xiii–xviii, 5, 11–12, 14, 17, 20–23, 27–33, 35–45, 47–50, 54–60, 62, 64–65, 67–68, 70, 78–81, 83–86, 90–108, 110–111, 115, 119–122, 125–131, 137–138, 140, 142–144, 146
Gospel x, xiii–xiv, xvi, xviii, 1, 9, 15–17, 22, 26, 33, 35, 37–43, 45, 47, 52–53, 57, 65, 71, 91,

93–94, 101–103, 107–108, 110, 115, 124–125, 128, 136, 141, 143–144
Graham, Billy 20, 116
Grassley, Senator Charles 123
Gromacki, Robert G. 88, 91

H

Hades 67, 79, 84–85
Hagah 97
Hagin, Kenneth ix, xiv, xvii, 5–6, 8, 11, 13–14, 16, 26–29, 31, 40–41, 49–55, 61–62, 64–65, 71–73, 75, 77, 83, 89, 105, 117, 119–126, 137–138, 143
Hanegraaff, Hank 6, 9–10, 13, 18–21, 24, 32, 38, 47, 53–55, 69, 73, 75–80, 87, 89, 92, 99–100, 107, 116–117, 137
Harrison, Buddy 27
Harrison House Publishers 27
Hayes, Norvel xiv, 53
Healing ix, xvi–xvii, 2–3, 22, 26–28, 42–44, 46, 50–51, 54–59, 61–62, 67, 69, 89, 93, 102–105, 109, 112–113, 115, 128, 137–138, 140, 144
Heaven xiv, 34, 45, 64, 105
Hell xiv, xv, 22, 79–80, 84, 96
Henotheistic 100
Heresy 5, 18, 58, 114
Hickey, Marilyn xiv
Hiebert, Paul 107
Higher Criticism 110
Hinduism 101
Holiness 25, 61, 68
Holy Spirit x, 1, 35, 49, 67, 79, 89, 115, 119, 127, 130, 132
Housworth, Ruth Kenyon 65

Hunt, Dave 3, 6–7, 37, 52, 112, 137–139
Hyatt, Eddie 60

I

ICFM 27, 49–50, 52, 76, 104
Irenaeus 6, 56–57, 140

J

Jesus Died Spiritually JDS 83, 87–89, 92

K

Kenyon, E. W. 6, 8–10, 13–14, 16–18, 25–26, 41, 52–55, 61, 63–73, 75–77, 80, 82–89, 92, 100, 109, 111, 117, 136
Kierkegaard, Søren 4
Kingdom 20, 32, 43–46, 61, 105, 110, 124–125, 127, 138, 143
Kirk, Andrew J. 93
Kraft, Charles 2, 11, 44, 48, 93–94, 110–112, 143

L

Lambert, M. D. 45
Lane, Mark H. 47
Liberal 4, 7, 43, 56, 71, 103, 105, 108, 110, 116, 133, 139
Lindsay, Gordon 27
Little gods 99–100
Love vii, x, xviii, 21, 29–30, 32, 40, 46, 50, 66, 81, 103–106, 116, 125–127, 129–132, 144
Love walk 29, 50, 105
Luther, Martin 6, 59–61, 75, 81–82, 84–85, 95, 140
Lutzer, Erwin W. 88

M

Martyr, Justin 6, 56, 105, 140
McArthur, John 94, 107, 112–113, 115–116
McConnell, Daniel 3, 6–7, 9–10, 13–20, 24, 26, 38, 47–48, 52–55, 57, 61, 63–71, 73, 76–79, 85, 87–89, 92, 94, 104, 107, 112, 114, 116–117, 119, 128, 137, 139
McIntyre, Joe E. 25, 47, 63, 66–70, 72, 85–88
McPherson, Aimee Semple 25
Melanchthon, Phillip 60
Metaphysical cults 6, 8, 10, 13–14, 16–17, 25–26, 54–55, 63, 65, 67, 69–71, 73, 77, 87, 89, 100, 107, 116–117, 136
Metaphysics 17, 21, 25, 47, 63, 65, 67–70, 87, 114
Methodist 25, 59, 61, 68, 94
Meyer, Joyce ix, xiv, 53, 123
Mfonobong, Nsehe 108
Middle Ages 80
Miracle 60, 94, 101–102, 125
Missio Dei 107
Mormonism 7, 65, 139
Mozambique 38, 45, 109
Mythology ix, xviii, 1, 4–10, 12–26, 38, 47, 52, 54–55, 61, 63, 65, 67, 69–71, 73, 76–77, 79, 86, 88–89, 92, 107, 109, 114, 117, 119, 131–132, 136–139, 143

N

New Age Movement 3, 138
Newbigin, Lesslie 38
New Covenant 26, 36, 38, 42, 136
New Covenant 26, 36, 38, 42
Newman, Martin vii, xv, 141
New Thought Metaphysics 65, 68
Nicklaus, Jack 97–98, 145
Ninety-five Theses 60
Nixon, President Richard 39
Nussbaum, Stan 2, 43, 94, 110–112

O

Oral Roberts University 16, 61, 63, 119
Origen 6, 18, 57, 78
Orthodox 6, 20, 77–78, 100
Osborn, T. L. x, xiv, 27, 51
Osteen, Dodi 53, 97, 104–105, 129
Oyedepo, David O. xiv, 53, 108–109

P

Penal Substitution 12, 74, 78, 80, 82–86, 124, 138
Pentecostal x, 10–11, 14, 25, 46, 51, 53–54, 61–62, 64, 70, 73, 107, 141
Perriman Report 7–8
Peters, Justin 3, 6–7, 10, 21–24, 38, 47, 57–59, 73, 92, 94, 107, 112–115, 136–139
Pink, A. W. 88
Plagiarizing 16, 64
Planck, Max 69
Platonism 68
Polycarp 56, 140
Potter, Philip 94
Pousson, Edward K. 40
Poverty xvii, 31, 35, 37–38, 40–45, 47–48, 50, 94, 121–122, 124, 130
Price, Fred xiv

Prince, Derek 58, 114
Prosperity xvii, 4, 7, 11, 23, 29–48, 50, 52, 70, 72–73, 93–94, 96–97, 99, 109, 120–122, 124–127, 139–140, 142, 144
Protestant Orthodoxy 12, 74, 81–82

R

Ransom Theory 80
Reformation 17, 60, 81
Rhema ix, 27, 40, 52, 65, 119
Rhema Bible Training Center 65
RMAI 27, 49, 52
Roberts, Oral 16, 22, 27, 38, 40–41, 51, 61, 63, 119
Ryrie, Charles Caldwell 88

S

Saint Augustine 13
Satan 35, 67, 69, 78, 84, 86, 120, 130
Savage, Minot J. 66
Savelle, Jerry 69
Secular xvii, 39, 48, 139
Senate Finance Committee 123
Shakespeare, William 24
Sherlock, Charles 94
Sickness 42–43, 50, 67, 69, 89, 104, 125, 129–130, 143
Socioeconomic 95
Sophists 81
Soteriological 85
Spiritual snobbery 7, 48, 131
Spurgeon, Charles 58
Stegall, Tom 90
Supernatural x, xiv, xvii–xviii, 1–4, 6–7, 9, 11, 42–44, 48, 50, 53–55, 57–61, 80, 93–95, 99, 101, 103–104, 110–111, 113, 115–116, 120–121, 129, 136–140, 142, 144
Supracultural 112, 124
Suprgeon, Charles 6, 58–59, 61, 140
Swatos Jr., William H. 47–48
Swedenborgianism 68
Syncretism 70

T

Taylor, Michael 39
Televangelism 47
Tertullian 6, 56, 140
The Christian Research Institute 20, 24, 116
The Enlightenment xvii, 71, 93
The Midas Touch 31, 121–122, 138
Theosis 100
Third-World 43
Tillich, Paul 4
Tilton, Robert xiv, 53, 80
Tongues x, 1, 22, 49, 53, 57, 113, 115, 132, 137–138
Transcendentalism 66, 68
Trine, Ralph Waldo 70

U

Unitarianism 66

W

Wealth xvii, 29, 31, 35, 37, 42, 44–45, 47, 52, 93–94, 121, 125–126
Wesley, Charles 51
Wesley, John 31, 46, 59, 61, 113
Whitfield, George 51
Wigglesworth, Smith xi, xviii, 62
Winston, Bill xiv, 52–53

Word of Faith ix–x, xiii–xiv, xvi–xviii, 1–22, 24–35, 37–41, 43–44, 46–48, 50–63, 65, 67, 69–83, 86–89, 92–93, 95, 99–101, 103–105, 107–114, 116–121, 123–126, 128–133, 136–140, 143–144
Word of God ix, xiv, xvi–xvii, 31–32, 34–35, 37, 49, 80, 96–97, 101, 104, 118, 138, 142–143
Wright, Bishop Tom 44

Y

Young, William xiii, 55–57

Index of Texts

Genesis
  1:3 95
  2:7 90
  2:17 90–91
  3:8–10 90
  5:5 90
  12:2-3 35, 51
  32:28 40
Deuteronomy
  8:17-18 31
  28:11-12 31
Joshua
  1:8 96, 142
Psalm
  22:1 90–91
  82:6 100
Proverbs
  8:21 40
  10:22 41, 43, 126
  19:17 122
  24:3-4 127
Isaiah
  53:4-5 128
  53:9 88
  53:10–12 89
  54:17 131
  61:3 114

Joel
  2:32 115
Matthew
  4:23 43
  6:10 45
  6:31-33 125
  6:33 127
  6:34 130
  8:13 128
  8:17 128
  12:36 96
  18:3 105
  19:26 98
  21:22 xiii, 28, 59, 96, 119, 128
  24:7 130
  27:46 90
Mark
  9:23 99
  10:25 32
  10:30 34, 38
  11:22-24 27, 95
  11:23 60, 105
  11:24 105
  16:15 143
  16:15-18 53
  16:17 115
  16:17-18 113, 115, 132

Luke
- 4:16-21 37
- 4:18 37
- 6:27-28 29, 105
- 6:38 33–34, 38, 126
- 12:10 132
- 23:46 91

John
- 2:1-11 125
- 9:25 xvi
- 10:10 118, 130, 136
- 10:33-35 99
- 12:8 122
- 12:33 88
- 13:34-35 106
- 14:12 115
- 14:26 130
- 15:17 99
- 16:24 xvi

Acts
- 1:8 115
- 5:1-2 130
- 13:8 18

Romans
- 1:10 22
- 1:17 75
- 4:17b 60, 95
- 5:17 100
- 6:23 91
- 8:28 130
- 8:35-39 131
- 10:10 96
- 11:36 21
- 12:1-2 36
- 13:8 30, 50
- 16:17 22

1 Corinthians
- 3:13 133
- 13: 4-8a 106
- 15:57 vii

- 16:2 23

2 Corinthians
- 5:20 100
- 5:21 90
- 8:9 42
- 9:6-8 127

Galatians
- 2:20 100
- 3:6-9 35
- 3:13-14 34, 42, 51
- 3:14 42
- 5:6 106
- 6:4-5 133

Ephesians
- 2:1-3 92
- 2:6 124
- 4:1-6 144
- 4:15 132
- 5:17 119

Philippians
- 2:2 xviii
- 4:6-7 41
- 4:13 99

1 Thessalonians
- 3:23 99

1 Timothy
- 6:5-10 126
- 6:6-11 33

2 Timothy
- 2:15 142
- 3:5 43, 115
- 3:16-17 130
- 4:2 5, 10, 55, 132
- 4:4 1

Hebrews
- 4:12 xvi, 108
- 5:7 91

James
- 1:25 105
- 3:17 11, 55

4:1-10 130
1 Peter
   2:2 35
   2:24 128
   3:18-20 79
2 Peter
   3:17 132
1 John
   1:6 21
3 John
   2 22–23, 41, 122–123

Selected Bibliography

Anderson, Digby, ed., *The Kindness that Kills*, S.P.C.K., London, 1984.

Atkinson, David, J., & Field David, H., eds., *New Dictionary of Christianity Ethics and Pastoral Theology*, Illinois, Inter Varsity Press, 1995.

Aulén, Gustaf, *Christus Victor: A Historical Sudy of the Three Types of the Idea of the Atonement*, London, S.P.C.K., 1965.

Barron, Bruce, *The Health and Wealth Gospel: What's Going on Today in a Movement That Has Shaped the Faith of Millions*, Intervarsity Press, U.S.A.,1987.

Barry, F., R., *The Atonement*, Great Britain, Hodder and Stoughton, 1968.

Beasley-Murray, G., R., *Jesus and the Kingdom of God*, U.S.A., Eerdmans, 1996.

Biblehub.com. (2019). *John 10 Barnes' Notes*. [online] Available at: https://biblehub.com/commentaries/barnes/john/10.htm [Accessed 18 Jun. 2019].

Biblehub.com. (2019). *3 John 1 Barnes' Notes*. [online] Available from: https://biblehub.com/commentaries/barnes/3_john/1.htm [Accessed 3 June 2019].

Bin, Tan, Che, Van Engen, Charles, & Gilliland, Dean, S., & Pierson, Paul, eds., *The Good News Of The Kingdom: Mission Theology For The Third Millennium*, Orbis Books, Maryknoll,1993.

Brown, Tom, *How To Receive From God: 10 Steps To Living in Victory*, Tom Brown Ministries, Texas, 2005.

Blomberg, Craig, L., *Neither Poverty nor Riches: A Biblical Theology of Possessions*, England, I.V.P., 1999.

Bosch, J., David, *Transforming Mission: Paradigm Shifts In Theology of Mission*, U.S.A., Orbis Books, 1991.

Bowler, Kate, *Blessed: A History of the American Prosperity Gospel,* U.S.A., Oxford University Press, 2013.

Bowman Jr., Robert, M., *Orthodoxy and Heresy,* Grand Rapids, Baker Books, 1992.

Bowman Jr., Robert, M., *The Word-Faith Controversy: Understanding the Health and Wealth Gospel,* Grand Rapids, Baker Books, 2001.

Bria, Ion, *Go Forth in Peace: Orthodox Perspectives on Mission,* Geneva, World Council of Churches Publications, 1992.

Broadhead, Edwin K. *"Implicit Christology and the Historical Jesus".* In Holmén, Tom; Porter, Stanley E. (eds.). *Handbook for the Study of the Historical Jesus.* Netherlands, Brill. 2011.

Brown, David, Rodd, Cyril, S., Ed, *New Occasions Teach New Duties? Christian Ethics for Today,* Edinburgh, T&T Clark, 1995.

Burkett, Delbert. *An introduction to the New Testament and the origins of Christianity,* Cambridge University Press, 2002.

Byrne, Peter, Ed., *Religious Studies* Volume 42 number 3, United Kingdom, Cambridge University Press, September 2006.

John Calvin, *The Institutes of the Christian Religion,* trans. Henry Beveridge (Edinburgh: Calvin Translation Society, 1846). 2 volumes in 1. 29/05/2019.

Campolo, Tony, *Revolution and Renewal: How Churches are Saving our Cities,* Louisville, John Knox Press, 2000.

Carriker, Timothy, C., Van Engen, Charles, & Gilliland, Dean, S., & Pierson, Paul, eds., *The Good News Of The Kingdom: Mission Theology For The Third Millennium,* Orbis Books, Maryknoll,1993.

Chadwick, Henry, *The Oxford History of Christianity,* Oxford University Press, Great Britain, 1993.

Clarke, Paul, Barry, and Linzey, Andrew, eds., *Dictionary of Ethics, Theology and Society,* Great Britain, Routledge, 1996.

Coleman, Simon, *The Globalization of Charismatic Christianity: Spreading the Gospel of Prosperity,* Cambridge, Cambridge University Press, 2001.

Collinson, Patrick, *The Oxford History of Christianity,* Oxford University Press, Great Britain, 1993.

Conn, Harvie, M., Ortiz, Manuel, eds., *The Kingdom, the City and the People of God: Urban Ministry,* I.V.P., United States of America, 2001.

Conn, Harvie, Van Engen, Charles, & Gilliland, Dean, S., & Pierson, Paul, eds., *The Good News Of The Kingdom: Mission Theology For The Third Millennium,* Orbis Books, Maryknoll,1993.

Copeland, Kenneth, *The Laws of Prosperity*, Kenneth Copeland Publications, Fort Worth,.1974.

Copeland, Kenneth, *Honor: Walking in Honesty, Truth, and Integrity*, U.S.A. Harrison House, 1992.

Copeland, Kenneth, *Prosperity: The Choice is Yours*, Kenneth Copeland Publications, Fort Worth, 1985.

Copeland, Kenneth, *The Blessing of The LORD Makes Rich and He Adds No Sorrow With It Proverbs 10:22*, Kenneth Copeland Publications, Fort Worth, 2011.

Copeland, Kenneth, *Honor: Walking in Honesty, Truth, and Integrity*, U.S.A. Harrison House, 1992.

Cotterell, Peter, *Mission and Meaninglessness: The Good News in a world of suffering and disorder*, Great Britain, SPCK, 1990.

Cross, F. L., Livingstone, E. A., *The Oxford Dictionary of the Christian Church*, Great Britain, Onford University Press, 2005.

Gilliland, Dean, "Contextualization," in *The Evangelical Dictionary of World Missions*, edited by Scott Moreau, Grand Rapids, MI: Baker Academic, 2000.

DeArteaga, W., L., *Quenching the Spirit*, U.S.A., Charisma House, [1992] 1996.

De Arteaga, W., L., 2003. Glenn Clark's Camps Furthest Out: The Schoolhouse of the Charismatic Renewal, *Pneuma*, SAGE Publications, Vol. 25. pp. 265-288.

Dillistone, F., W., *A Christian Understanding of Atonement*, Great Britain, S.C.M.P. 1984.

EFCA, https://www.efca.org/resources/document/efca-statement-faithElliott.

Cullis, Charles, *Comfortable Compassion: Poverty, Power and the Church*, London, Hodder and Stoughton, 1987.

Fahrenholz, Geiko, Muller, *The Kingdom and the Power: The Theology of Jurgen Moltmann*, SCM Press, London, 2000.

Fee, Gordon, D., *The Disease of the Health and Wealth Gospels*, Vancouver, Regent College Publishing, 2006.

Finney, Charles, G., *Revival Lectures*, Grand Rapids: Flemming H. Revell Co, 1993.

Fodor, Jim, ed., Modern Theology, Volume 23, Number 4, U.S.A., Blackwell Publishing, October 2007.

Gensichen, Hans-Werner, & Scherer, J. A., *The Encyclopaedia of Christianity Volume 3*, Grand Rapids, Eerdmans, 2003.

Gorringe, Timothy, *God's Just Vengeance*, Great Britain, Cambridge University Press, 1996.

Gromacki, Robert, *Stand Bold in Grace: An Exposition of Hebrews*, The Woodlands, TX: Kress, 2002.

Gunton, Colin, E., *The Actuality of Atonement: A Study of Metaphor, Rationality and the Christian Tradition*, Edinburgh, T & T Clark, 1988.

Hagin, Kenneth, E., *Healing Belongs to Us*, Tulsa, Faith Library Publications, 1991.

Hagin, Kenneth, E., *Redeemed from Poverty, Sickness, and Spiritual Death*, Tulsa, Faith Library Publications, 1983

Hagin, Kenneth, E., *How To Write Your Own Ticket With God*, Tulsa, RHEMA Bible Church, 1979.

Hagin, Kenneth, *How to Turn Your Faith Loose*, Tulsa, Faith Library Publications, 1978.

Hagin, Kenneth, E., *Love: The Way to Victory*, U.S.A., Faith Library Publications, 2005.

Hagin, Keneth, E., *The Midas Touch*, U.S.A., Faith Library Publications, Tulsa, 2000.

Hagin, Kenneth, E., *Zoe: The God Kind of Life*, U.S.A., Faith Library Publications, 1993.

Hagin, Kenneth, E., *The Believer's Authority*, Tulsa, RHEMA Bible Church, 1984.

Hagin, Kenneth, E., *Biblical Keys to Financial Prosperity*, Tulsa, RHEMA Bible Church, 1995.

Kenneth, Hagin, 1997, Luther on Atonement-Reconfigured, *Concordia Theological Quarterly*, SAGE Publications, Volume 61, Number 4, pp. 251-276.

Hagin, Kenneth, E., *Why Do People Fall Under the Power* Classic Favorites Series (Tulsa: Kenneth Hagin Ministries, 1976), Audio Tape 17H06.

Hanegraaff, Hank, *Christianity in Crisis*, Oregon, Word Publishing, 1993.

Hanegraaff, Hank, *Counterfeit Revival: Looking For God In All The Wrong Places*, U.S.A., Word Publishing, 1997.

Healing and Revival, 2019, *Preaching Prayer and Compassion*, Available at: https://healingandrevival.com/BioCHSpurgeon.htm. [Accessed 8 June 2019].

Hiebert, Paul, The Gospel in Human Contexts: Changing Perceptions of Contextualization, in *MissionShift,* edited by David Hesselgrave and Ed Stetzer Nashville, TN, Broadman & Holman, 2010.

Hoedemaker, L. A., Verstraelen, F. J., ed, *Missiology: An Ecumenical Introduction,* Eardmans, Grand Rapids U.S.A. 1995.

Holy Bible, King James Version, Grand Rapids, Zondervan, 1994.

Hunt, Dave, *The Seduction of Christianity,* Harvest House Publishing, U.S.A., 1985.

Hunt S., 'Magical Moments: An Intellectualist Approach to the Neo-Pentecostal Faith Ministries', Religion 28:271-280, 1998.

Hyatt, Eddie *How-martin-luther-gained-the-faith-for-supernatural-miracles.* [ONLINE] Available at: https://www.charismamag.com. [Accessed 16 July 2018].

Irenaeus, *Ante Nicene Fathers vol 1: Irenaeus Against Heresies,* Book 2, ch. 32, sec. 4, p. 847.

Jackson, R., 1989, Prosperity theology and the faith movement, *Themelios,* Volume 15, pp.16-24.

Jacob, W. M., ed., *Theology,* Volume CX, Number 858 November/December 2007, London, S.P.C.K.

Jennings, Daniel, R., *The Supernatural Occurrences of John Wesley,* Sean Multimedia, 2005.

Kaiser, Walter C. Jr., *The Old Testament Case for Material Blessings and the Contemporary Believer,* The Gospel and Contemporary Perspectives, Douglas Moo, ed., Grand Rapids, Kregel Publications, 1997.

Kenyon's (2018), [online] http://www.kenyons.org/index.html Available at: http://www.kenyons.org/plagiarism-of-ew-kenyons.html [Accessed 12 June 2018].

Kenyon's (2018), [online] http://www.kenyons.org/index.html Available at: http://www.kenyons.org/metaphysical-cults.html [Accessed 7th July 2018].

Kenyon, E., W., *Jesus the Healer,* Lynnwood USA, Kenyon's Gospel Publishing Society, 1943.

Kenyon, E. W., *What happened from the cross to the throne,* Lynnwood USA, Kenyon's Gospel Publishing Society, 1945.

Kenyon, E., W., *The Hidden Man,* Washington, Kenyon Publishing Society, [1945] 1998a.

Kenyon, E., W., *The Two Kinds of Faith: Faith's Secrets Revealed,* Seattle, Kenyon's Gospel Publishing Company, 1942.

Kenyon, E. W., *Identification: A Romance In Redemption*, Lynnwood, USA, Kenyon's Gospel Publishing Society, [1946] 1998.

Kenyon, E. W., *In His Presence*, Lynnwood USA, Kenyon's Gospel Publishing Society, 2004.

King, Paul, L. 2018. *A B Simpson and the modern faith movement.* [ONLINE] Available at: https://www.hopefaithprayer.com/word-of-faith/a-b-simpson-and-the-modern-faith-movement-paul-l-king/. [Accessed 26 June 2018].

Kirk, Andrew, J., Vanhoozer, Kevin, J., eds., *To Stake a Claim*, New York, Orbis Books, 1999.

Kirk, Andrew J., *What is Mission? Theological Explorations*, London, Darton, Longman and Todd, 1999.

Kraft, Charles, H., *Anthropology for Christian Witness*, New York, Orbis Books, 1996.

Lambert, M. D., *Franciscan Poverty*, London, S.P.C.K., 1961.

Lane, Mark, H. "John Wesley Receives the Holy Spirit at Aldersgate" (PDF). Bible Numbers for Life. Retrieved 3rd July 2018.

Lie, Geir, 1996, E W Kenyon : Cult Founder or Evangelical Minister? *Journal of the European Pentecostal Theological Association*, SAGE Publications, Volume 16, pp. 71-86.

Lie, Geir, 2000, The Theology of E. W. Kenyon: Plain Heresy or Within the Boundaries of Pentecostal-Charismatic "Orthodoxy"? U.S.A., *Pneuma*, SAGE Publications, Volume 22, Number 1, pp. 85-114.

Livingstone, E. A., ed., *The Oxford Dictionary of The Christian Church*, New York, Oxford University Press, 1997.

Lutzer, Erwin W., *Cries from the Cross*, Chicago, Moody, 2002.

McConnell, D., R., *A Different Gospel*, U.S.A., Hendrickson Press, 1988.

McConnell, D., R., *A Different Gospel*, U.S.A., Hendrickson Press, 1995.

McFague, Sallie, *Life Abundant: Rethinking Theology and Economy for a Planet in Peril*, Minneapolis, Fortress Press, 2000.

McIntyre, Joe, *E. W. Kenyon The True Story*, Charisma House, U.S.A., 1997.

McManners, John, ed., Clement of Alexandria,'*The Oxford History of Christianity*' Oxford University Press, England, 1990.

Mfonobong, Nsehe. 2011. *The Five Richest Pastors in Nigeria,*. [ONLINE] Available at: https://www.forbes.com. [Accessed 10 July 2018].

Miller D. E., *Reinventing American Protestantism: Christianity in the New Millennium*, Berkley, University of California Press, 1997

Morris, L., L., ed., *New Dictionary of Theology*, London, I.V.P., 1993.

Morrow, T., W., J., ed., *New Dictionary of Theology*, London, I.V.P., 1993.

Myconius, Friedrich, Encyclopædia Britannica (11th ed.). 1911.

Newbigin, Lesslie, *The Open Secret: An Introduction to the Theology of Mission*, S.P.C.K., Great Britain, 1995.

Newbigin, Lesslie, *Foolishness to the Greeks*, London, S.P.C.K., 1986.

Nussbaum, Stan, *A Readers Guide to Transforming Mission,* U.S.A., Orbis Books, 2005.

Orwell, 2018, *Orwell on Truth by George Orwell,* [ONLINE] Available at: https://www.penguin.co.uk/books/1114450/orwell-on-truth/ [Accessed 5 July 2018].

Osteen, Dodie, *Healed of Cancer*, Lakewood Church, U.S.A., 1986.

Orr, James. "The Apostles' Creed" *International Standard Bible Encyclopedia*. Reformed. Archived from the original on June 22, 2011. Retrieved May 19, 2011.

Pattison, Stephen, *The Faith of the Managers: When Management Becomes Religion*, London, Cassell, 1997.

Pentecost, J. Dwight, *A Faith That Endures,* Grand Rapids, Discovery House, 1992.

Percy, Martyn, *Power and the Church*, Cassell, London, 1998.

Perriman, Andrew, ed., *Faith Health and Prosperity*, Paternoster Press, U.K., 2003.

Peters, Justin, *http://justinpeters.org/a-call-for-discernment/.* [online] Available at: http://justinpeters.org. [Accessed 19 July 2018] 2018.

Peters, Justin, *Personal Testimony,* Justin Peters Ministries, Available at: https://justinpeters.org/personal-testimony/ [Accessed June 3, 2019].

Prince, Derek, *Spiritual Warfare For The End Times: How To Defeat The Enemy*, Chosen a division of Baker Publishing Group, Minnesota USA, 2017.

Pousson, Edward, K., *Spreading the Flame,* Grand Rapids, Zondervan Publications, 1992.

Pulitzer, Atlas of Pentecostalism, Available at:

https://pulitzercenter.org/projects/africa-nigeria-pentecostal-christians-holy-spirit-global-religion-iconography-cartography-data-visualization [Accessed 6th July 2018].

Robert, Dana, Van Engen, Charles, & Gilliland, Dean, S., & Pierson, Paul, eds., *The Good News Of The Kingdom: Mission Theology For The Third Millennium*, Orbis Books, Maryknoll,1993.

Roberts, Oral, *My Favorite Bible Scriptures*, Tulsa, Oral Roberts Evangelist Association, 1963.

Ryrie, Charles Caldwell, *Biblical Theology of the New Testament*, Chicago, Moody, 1959.

Sedgwick, Peter, *The Enterprise Culture*, London, S.P.C.K., 1992.

Segal, Robert, E., Ryba, Thomas, eds., Religion, Volume 37, Issue 2, Elsevier Publishing, U.K., June 2007.

Selby, Peter, *Grace and Mortgage: The Language of Grace and the Debt of the World*, London, Darton, Longman and Todd Ltd., 1997.

Shenk, Wilbert, R, *Changing Frontiers of Mission*, New York, Orbis, 1999.

Shenk, Wilbert, R, ed, *Exploring Church Growth*, Grand Rapids, Eerdmans, 1983.

Sheppard, David, *Bias to the Poor*, Hodder and Stoughton, London, 1983.

Sherlock, Charles, *The Doctrine of Humanity: Contours of Christian Theology*, U.S.A., I.V.P., 1996.

Simmons, Dale, *E.W.Kenyon and the Postbellum Pursuit of Peace, Power and Plenty*, U.S.A., Scarecrow Press, 1996.

Simpson, William, M., R., 2007, The Significance of Andrew Perriman's Faith, Health and Prosperity in the Word of Faith Debate, *Journal of Pentecostal Theology*, SAGE Publications, Vol. 16, No. 1, pp.64-96.

Singh-Kurtz, S. and Kopf, D. (2019). The US witch population has seen an astronomical rise. [online] Quartzy. Available at: https://qz.com/quartzy/1411909/the-explosive-growth-of-witches-wiccans-and-pagans-in-the-us/ [Accessed 20 Jul. 2019].

Spurgeon, http://charismatamatters.blogspot.com/2013/07/quotes-on-divine-healing.html [ONLINE] Available at: https://www.charismatamatters.blogspot.com. [Accessed 16 July 2018].

Stacey, John, *Groundwork of Theology*, Epworth Press, London, 1994.

Stegall, Tom, 2018. *Grace Family Journal*. [ONLINE] Available at: http://www.gracegospelpress.org/did-christ-die-spiritually-and-physically/. [Accessed 21 June 2018].

Sugden, C. M. N., *New Dictionary of Theology*, Inter Varsity Press, England, 1988.

Swatos Jr., William, H., ed., *Encyclopaedia of Religion and Society*, U.S.A., Altamira Press, 1998.

Taylor, Michael, *Christianity, Poverty and Wealth*, Great Britain, S.P.C.K., 2003.

The Book of Common Prayer, Vulcan hammer, Archived, from the original on May 16, 2011. Retrieved May 19, 2011.

Thiselton, A., C., ed. *New Dictionary of Theology*, London, I.V.P., 1993.

Van Engen, Charles, Van Engen, Charles, & Gilliland, Dean, S., & Pierson, Paul, eds., *The Good News Of The Kingdom: Mission Theology For The Third Millennium*, Orbis Books, Maryknoll,1993.

Vanderkam, James, C. ed. Journal of Biblical Literature, Volume 126, Number 3, Fall 2007.

Verstraelen, F. J. ed. *Missiology: An Ecumenical Introduction*, Eardmans, Grand Rapids U.S.A. 1995.

Walvoord, John F., *Matthew: Thy Kingdom Come*, Chicago, Moody, 1974.

Warrington, Keith, *Healing and Suffering: Biblical and Pastoral Reflections*, Milton Keynes, Paternoster Press, 2005.

Warrington, Keith, 1997, The Use of the Name (of Jesus) in Healing and Exorcism with partial reference to the teachings of Kenneth Hagin, Great Britain, *Journal of the European Pentecostal Theological Association,* SAGE Publications, Number 17, pp.16-36.

Weaver, Denny, J., *The Non Violent Atonement*, U.S.A., Eardmans Publishing Company, 2001.

Wiersbe, W., *Wycliffe Handbook of Preaching and Preachers*, Moody Press, U.S.A., 1984.

Wigglesworth, Smith, *Ever Increasing Faith Revised Edition*, Springfield, Missouri, Gospel Publishing House, 1924.

Wingate, Douglas, J., *Divine Faith And Miracles*, Florida, Life Christian University Press, 2010.

Woodbridge, John, D., Biblical Authority: A Critique of the Rogers/McKim Proposal, Grand Rapids, Zondervan,1982.

Wright, D. F., *New Dictionary of Theology*, Inter Varsity Press, England, 1993.

Wright, Tom, *Simply Christian*, S.P.C.K., England, 2006.

Yates, Timothy, *The Expansion of Christianity*, Lion Publishing, China, 2004.

Yates, Timothy, *Mission: An Invitation To God's Future*, Derby, Cliff College Publishing, 2000.

Young, William, *Miracles in Church History*. [online] Available at: https://biblicalstudies.org.uk/pdf/churchman/102-02_102.pdf. [Accessed 20 July 2018].

Youtubecom. 2019. YouTube. [Online]. [3 June 2019]. Available from: https://www.youtube.com/watch?v=ofqhbBEDvC8

About the Author

Bishop Dr. Steven Lyn Evans left his home in South Wales as a young 20-year-old with a prayer and a dream to become a singer. Within four days he was singing on the stage of the world-famous London Palladium. In 1996 whilst performing at the Royal Variety Show, God used a conversation with fellow Welshman and singer Tom Jones, to convict him that his 'calling' was to preach the Gospel of Jesus Christ.

He is Lead Pastor of Living Faith Church in Greater Manchester and is also the Presiding Bishop of The International Christian Church Network (TICCN).

His ministry gained widespread attention due to the many miracles of God following. Testimonies of these were featured on front page secular newspaper headlines in Great Britain.

Steven testifies to the need for bible believing Christians to compromise their minds to the Word of God rather than compromising the Word of God to the limits of human understanding.

Steven Lyn Evans
Ministries

For further information on this publication visit:
www.stevenlynevansministries.org

CPSIA information can be obtained
at www.ICGtesting.com
Printed in the USA
BVHW071556100919
558045BV00003B/351/P